When  in Doubt,

Ask for More

When in Doubt,
Ask for More

And 213 Other
Life and Career Lessons
for the Mission-Driven Leader

Alex Counts

Rivertowns
BOOKS

Printed in the United States of America
March, 2020

ISBN-13: 978-0-9790080-7-8
ISBN-10: 0-9790080-7-7
LCCN Imprint Name: Rivertowns Books

Rivertowns Books are available online from Amazon as well as from bookstores and other retailers. Requests for information and other correspondence may be addressed to:

Rivertowns Books
240 Locust Lane
Irvington NY 10533
Email: info@rivertownsbooks.com

Contents

Introduction

ONE EVENING IN JULY, 2016, when I was struggling with several writing projects—including one that would become this book—I headed out for a jog along Manhattan's East River. A creature of habit, I took the exact same five-mile route I had used for years.

It was a rather solitary exercise, as there were few other runners or bikers due to threatening skies. I liked that. Running for me has always been a combination of exercise and meditation; I eschew partners to converse with as well as earphones to pipe in music.

As I turned around and began to backtrack to our family apartment on East 81st Street, it started to rain. I don't mind a light drizzle when I'm running; in fact, it can be quite refreshing. But when it becomes a driving rain, as it did that evening, it's not pleasant.

Then the thunder began. I began thinking, somewhat morbidly, about the possibility of being struck by lightning as I ran. I tried to steer closer to nearby trees and buildings to protect myself. And as I scampered back toward safety, I pondered what my regrets would be if I were to suddenly expire that night.

It was an intriguing question, like many I pondered during my jogs. It spurred other questions. How prepared was I to die? I'd completed my will and estate plan. I hadn't written up instructions for my funeral, but I suspected that my wife Emily would do something appropriate. I could think of no unspoken expressions of love or requests for forgiveness to deliver to anyone close to me.

However, I realized that I'd have one major regret if my life were to end that night. Over the previous decades, I'd learned a lot about living a life dedicated to making the world a better place, including the challenges of caring for oneself while pursuing a career in public service. But I had never catalogued those lessons for the benefit of those who would someday follow me.

Not that I'd kept all of my insights completely secret. During my forties, I'd begun to share some of them with a handful of people I was mentoring. Some found them meaningful, which meant a great deal to me. But most of my life and work lessons had never been passed along to anyone else. I realized that, unless I took the time to write them down, they'd die with me. I found that thought depressing.

Writing this book became a kind of self-designed anti-depressant therapy for me. I am happy to report that it worked.

Learning to Be a Professional

"WE SHOULD JUST FOCUS on answering *that* question," she said to me matter-of-factly.

I was sitting in the office of a young lawyer named Jennifer Drogula at Wilmer, Cutler and Pickering, one of the country's most prestigious law firms. (Today it is known as WilmerHale.) I'd met Jennifer after boldly asking Paul Dwyer, a partner at her firm, to provide Grameen Foundation, which I headed, with pro bono legal counsel. I needed their advice in order to get closure on a complex, $10.6 million transaction with a large, New York-based foundation to benefit an exciting project launched by my Nobel laureate mentor, Professor Muhammad Yunus. (I describe the lessons for fundraising derived from that successful effort in some detail in chapter seven of my book *Changing the World Without Losing Your Mind.*)

When Paul asked me how much of his firm's time I might need, I guessed, "Around 15 hours." I was off by a mile. By the summer of 1998, the amount of time Paul and Jennifer had put into the project was in the hundreds of hours. I later learned that Jennifer found it one of the most exciting opportunities of her first decade as a lawyer.

On this particular day, I'd been explaining a tangle of complicated, interrelated issues to Jennifer, and now, as she so often did, she was cutting through the thicket to highlight the one key question at the heart of the matter.

As I contemplated Jennifer's latest insight, a couple of questions popped into my mind. One was, How was she able to see so clearly what I found complex and confusing? I was a reasonably intelligent person and about the same age as Jennifer, yet many things that seemed obvious to her were a mystery to me—not just technical or legal issues, but matters related to project management, negotiation, and the tactical and emotional aspects of business strategy. How did she do it?

Which led me to an even bigger, slightly embarrassing question: How had Jennifer learned to be such an effective professional? Had someone taught her? If so, who? Was it part of a law school class or an early-career internship? If she'd taken some class on how to be consistently effective in the workplace, it must have been one I skipped—since I didn't even know it existed.

Those questions kept percolating in the back of my mind throughout the afternoon. So at the end of our meeting that day, I decided to take advantage of my willingness to ask questions that might make me appear ignorant or inexperienced. "Jennifer," I said, "You're such a professional! You're so good at analyzing complex situations and seeing the best way to move forward. How did you learn that?"

It was an odd sort of question, so it's not surprising that Jennifer struggled to answer it. She and I talked more about our tactical options over the next few weeks. About a month later, the negotiations broke down entirely, and I thought the deal might be dead. Jennifer then demonstrated pragmatic, proactive leadership by sending a perfectly-worded email to everyone involved. It served to jump-start the process, beginning a final series of negotiations that ended in success.

Watching Jennifer at work was a learning experience for me. During one conference call near the end, I led the conversation with a degree of confidence that I'd utterly lacked when the negotiations had begun in mid-1997. Slowly, I was becoming the kind of professional Jennifer already was.

I had many limitations during my early days as a leader, and still have a quite a few. But one of the ways I gradually improved my effectiveness as a leader was to be continually on the lookout for good ideas from people I worked with, competed with, observed from a distance, or considered mentors. If I saw something that worked well, I often tried it, even if it initially felt unnatural.

Here's an example. During the early part of my career in South Asia, I had absorbed from the local culture a reluctance to say thank you to people, especially workplace subordinates and consultants. I suppose it was out of a fear that praising others would make them complacent.

During my thirties, I got to know people on Grameen Foundation's board of directors like Susan Davis and Bob Eichfeld who never missed an opportunity to express gratitude and appreciation to me and to others. Doing so *didn't* appear to make me or anyone else self-satisfied or lazy. Rather, it gave us pleasure and if anything motivated us to do even better next time. I observed, learned, and began, awkwardly and fitfully at first, to change my default mode from being stingy with praise to being generous with it.

If I'd developed that habit earlier, Grameen Foundation and the people who worked there would have benefited a lot. If I'd never changed my posture, the organization and its mission would have suffered much more.

In the same way, many of the professional behaviors I observed in Jennifer became staples of my approach over time. In other cases, I simply distilled lessons from my own life, occasionally through accidentally doing something differently and being surprised and delighted at how well it turned out.

The most valuable of these lessons are the ones that appear in this book.

Passing Insights on to the Next Generation

KEN BAIN, A GREAT COLLEGE TEACHER who has authored several books on his craft, once wrote, "Teaching is one of the human endeavors that seldom benefits from its past. . . . For the most part, [great teachers'] insights die with them, and subsequent generations must discover anew the wisdom that drove their practices." I believe that the same is true for social entrepreneurship and nonprofit leadership.

My hope is that the various insights that populate this book will help a new generation of nonprofit leaders grow faster and accomplish more at reduced personal cost and with more joy. And given that so many people who have read *Changing the World Without Losing Your Mind* have found its lessons applicable to business, government service, academia, and even to parenting, I am optimistic that this book will also feel relevant to those who work outside the nonprofit sphere.

I've read and enjoyed a number of books by heads of nonprofits. But most of these books focus on what their authors have achieved. This book is different. It is rooted in what I *learned* in trying to heal the world, rather than what I *accomplished.* Often my most important lessons came from the kinds of traumatic and humiliating failures that most leaders, especially nonprofit executives, go to great lengths to keep hidden from the public, and even from themselves.

My goal in these pages is not to tell you what to do or not do. Rather, I am inviting you to overhear me, at age 52, having an extended conversation with myself in my late twenties, at the time I was gearing up for my first big leadership role as the founding CEO of Grameen Foundation. In that conversation, I share lessons that I would have benefited from learning much earlier.

It's up to you to pick and choose which ideas and techniques you want to adopt, try, modify, or ignore. I hope and expect that, in the process, you'll cobble together a list of practical experiments that will help you improve your current approach to work and life.

The lessons that appear in this volume are arranged alphabetically rather than thematically, in the style of Robert Townsend's classic management book *Up the Organization*, which I learned about through my publisher, Karl Weber of Rivertowns Books. This structure is designed to encourage serendipity: an insight about how to be an effective public speaker might follow one offering advice on getting enough rest while traveling for work and precede one about a little-known technique for successful fundraising. Living life in a learning mode has exactly that kind of random rhythm to it. Big ideas that may influence your entire outlook on life may strike you around the same time as a small but powerful tip that simply makes a day at work a little less stressful and a little more productive.

Feel free to read this book in any way that you find enjoyable, meaningful, and convenient. You might spend a few minutes scanning a handful of lessons over breakfast or on your commute to work each day. You might read the whole book in one gulp. Perhaps you could have your work team read it and then report on the ten lessons they already use, the ten they want to try, and then ten they would never, ever adopt—an interesting variation on the team-building ice-breaker concept.

Let me know how you use this book and the value you get out of it. I'm always thrilled to get messages from readers of my books, articles, and blog posts. My email address is alexcounts09@gmail.com, and I will respond.

Thanks for reading, and my best wishes for wherever your life and career journey may take you.

Alex Counts
Hyattsville, Maryland
January, 2020

Guide to the Icons

The lessons in this book fall into eight subject areas of importance to most nonprofit professionals. They're identified by the icons that appear at the beginning of each entry.

 *Board management*—lessons dealing with recruiting, nurturing, and leading an effective and productive board of directors.

 *Fundraising*—lessons that can help you tackle the challenges associated with fundraising with less stress and greater success.

 *Leadership*—lessons focused on issues of organizational management, from motivating and inspiring

employees to dealing with crises.

 *People skills*—lessons related to the human aspects of leadership, such as working constructively with difficult employees and forging strong connections with key stakeholders.

 *Personal wellness*—lessons in tending to your own physical, psychological, and spiritual well-being even as you dedicate you career to serving the needs of society.

 *Public speaking*—lessons on how to be clear, persuasive, inspiring, and less anxious when you have the opportunity to share your message with the world.

 *Running a meeting*—lessons that can help you make the meetings you run or participate in more efficient

and less frustrating for everyone.

 *Travel*—lessons in surviving and even thriving while navigating the often stressful demands of traveling on behalf of your organization.

The Lessons

Accepting Applause

 ONE ELEMENT OF PUBLIC GRACE is the ability to be comfortable while accepting a compliment. A parallel skill is the ability to accept, and indeed to enjoy, the applause of an audience. When you finish delivering a speech, be sure to stay on stage and maintain eye contact with the audience while they applaud for you. This applies especially if the event has been arranged wholly or partially in your honor, or if the audience accords you a standing ovation. Avoid the mistake of hurrying off stage, which deprives the audience of the satisfaction of knowing you are accepting and savoring their appreciation.

Advance Travel Connections, Making

HAVING TO TRAVEL A LOT is one of the most stressful and difficult aspects of many professional careers. Make something positive out of this potential negative by periodically looking a few weeks ahead in your calendar. Think about acquaintances, friends, and family who live in the places you'll be visiting in the next month or two. Then consider contacting them in advance to set up a time to get together. Remember, people with complicated lives (like yours) often can't make last-minute plans. So call or email them with an invitation. If they can make the time to see you, you'll enjoy a few moments of fun and friendship while you travel. And even if they can't, your relationship will have been renewed and strengthened.

Advice Is (Often) Unnecessary

 WHEN A COLLEAGUE, associate, or friend chooses to talk with you about some important and deeply personal issue they are wrestling with, don't assume they want your advice. They probably don't. Instead, your most valuable contribution is likely to be hearing them out, letting them know you understand their situation and feelings, and affirming your belief that they'll ultimately make the right decision about how to handle it. Offering those three simple gifts can often do more to ensure a happy outcome than the most well-intentioned advice in the world.

Affirmation—The 5x Rule

 WHEN CONSIDERING WHETHER or not to affirm a friend, colleague, family member, or stranger—for example, by offering a compliment, a thank-you, or a gesture of public appreciation—assume that your affirmation will be five times more meaningful for them than you instinctively believe it will be. My experience suggests that this assumption is likely to be accurate.

Agendas Are Made to Be Bent

 WHEN YOU'RE RUNNING a meeting, sticking to the schedule and the agenda are important priorities. But they are not *all-important.* During the meeting, you may discover that a particular conversation or topic is turning out to be unexpectedly urgent, complicated, or rewarding. When that happens, let the discussion go over time and find a way to make up for it later. You (and your team) will probably be glad you did.

Ambassadors for Your Organization—How to Manage Them

 ASKING INDIVIDUALS WHO are *not* part of your staff fundraising team to serve as organizational ambassadors by helping to spread the good word about your work can be a very effective strategy for growing your network of supporters. But you need to manage these ambassadors carefully. Make sure they receive the training they need, including current information about your work, your finances, the status of your mission, and so on. And be sure there is a clear understanding as to what you expect from your ambassadors and what they will receive in return—for example, in terms of support and recognition. Leaders of partner organizations (such as sub-grantees), for instance, may expect an equivalent gesture of support from you. Be businesslike about these details so that those who serve as ambassadors for you find it enjoyable and rewarding.

Apologies, Accepting

NOT EVERYONE HAS LEARNED or mastered the art of offering a heartfelt apology [*see* Apologizing: Make It Real]. This means that, when you've been wronged, you may sometimes find yourself on the receiving end of a watered-down, awkward, somewhat insincere, or otherwise imperfect apology. Rather than take offense, consider that the apologizer is probably doing their level best to deal with a situation they find painful and embarrassing. Accept the flawed apology graciously. It's a valuable step toward restoring a positive relationship for the future—or creating one for the first time.

Apologizing: Make It Real

 WHEN YOU MAKE A MISTAKE and need to apologize—as we all occasionally do— avoid cluttering and diluting your apology. An apology that includes the word "if" or "but" is often worse than saying nothing at all. As author Adam Grant puts it, "'I'm sorry if . . .' isn't an apology. It's an expression of doubt that you did anything wrong." Offer a real apology that takes full responsibility for your error, and then you'll be able to move on.

Approachable, Being

EVERY LEADER NEEDS to be accessible and approachable, but this is especially important in a nonprofit organization. When people are working at demanding jobs that are often underappreciated in our society and that usually pay less than similar employment in the for-profit realm, non-monetary forms of support are particularly important. So make it easy for people to connect with you. Take the initiative to talk with them regularly, individually and in small groups, to get a sense of what the organization looks like through their eyes. And aim to return calls and emails from them within two or three days (at the most) so that they can get your attention, advice, and decisions without delay.

"As This Morning's Speaker Said . . . "

ONE USEFUL TRICK for the speech maker is to take a moment early in your talk to mention something that was said or done earlier in the program. This serves a few purposes: It shows the audience that you are not merely reciting a canned stump speech; it links your message with ideas the audience may already be thinking about; and it shows that you are "one of the group," adding your contribution to an ongoing conversation, rather than parachuting in with a speech that may or may not be relevant.

The Ask: Keep It Simple

 WHEN YOU'RE READY to ask a potential major donor for funds for the first time, it is usually best to ask for something very specific. For example, you could say, "We're about to launch a one-million-dollar project that I think you'll find really interesting, and I'd like to invite you to be one of ten people to contribute $100,000 to make it possible." Alternatively, you could offer to co-create with them a specific project or sub-project that is tailored to their values and interests and is also consistent with your organization's mission and strategy. Avoid making a vague request or offering a menu of options. When your ask falls into the "muddy middle," it tends to confuse rather than motivate a potential donor.

Asking for Help When Traveling

 AS YOU GAIN EXPERIENCE with traveling for work, figure out the kinds of accommodations and conveniences that make your days more comfortable and enjoyable—a particular seat on the plane; a certain type of pillow for your hotel room; a quiet, radio-free taxi ride, or whatever. Once you know what makes a difference for you, ask for those things courteously and without any air of entitlement. You may be surprised how often you will get what you ask for.

Audience, Maybe It Was the

WHEN IT COMES TO public speaking, understand and appreciate that the effectiveness of a speech has as much to do with the quality of the *audience*—that is, their interest in the topic, their knowledge of the subject, and their affinity for the speaker and the speaker's ideas—as it does with the quality of the speech itself. With this reality in mind, don't take too much credit if your speech goes well, and don't beat yourself up too much if it does not. You—the speaker—were just half of the equation.

"Avoid Power Point" Is the Rule—But There Are Exceptions

 THERE ARE GOOD REASONS for all the groans and bitter jokes about Power Point presentations. Too often they serve as a crutch or a distraction, separating the speaker from the audience rather than connecting them. So avoid using slides except in one of these three exceptional cases: (1) Graphics are critical to making your key points, as in a talk about the details of the Federal budget. (2) Photos or other images can bring your topic to life, as in a speech about the glories of America's national parks. (3) Your audience is largely made up of people whose primary language is different from your own, in which case explanatory words and images may help bridge the comprehension gap.

Balancing Ego with Humility

 MOST PEOPLE ARE WELL aware of the trap of developing an excessive ego, much less megalomania. This a real risk for the leader of any successful organization, and almost everyone has known (and may have suffered under) leaders who have allowed out-of-control ego to undermine their ability to listen, learn, and grow. But fewer people are aware of the opposite danger— namely, the pitfall of excessive humility. Members of an organization want to be proud of their leaders, and they want to know that they are part of a well-led team that is accomplishing great things and is recognized for doing so. So don't trumpet your achievements too loudly or too frequently—but don't hide your light under a bushel, either.

The Balkanized Board

 MOST NONPROFIT ORGANIZATIONS have boards that don't work very well [*see* The Dysfunctional Nonprofit Board]. One relatively benign variation of this phenomenon is the board that is divided into spheres of influence, in which each board member focuses on one area of interest (say, Latin American programs) and doesn't pay much attention to any other part of the organization. My friend and mentor Susan Davis referred to this as a "Balkanized board." This kind of board may seem, at a glance, to be high-performing, since it features little overt conflict. But few if any of the members feel a sense of ownership of the entire enterprise, leaving it to the CEO to be the lonely champion of the organization as a whole. Look out for the phenomenon of Balkanization on your board, and fight against it by recruiting "generalist" board

members and encouraging them to learn about and support every area of the organization's work and think deeply about how all the pieces fit together.

Be Bold, But Be Grounded

 SELF-PROCLAIMED LEADERSHIP experts often tout the benefits of adopting so-called "Big Hairy Audacious Goals," which are alleged to inspire and motivate team members far more than modest objectives. Yes, this can work. But Big Hairy Audacious Goals can easily backfire, leading to cynicism if they are not sufficiently rooted in organizational and environmental realities. Experience suggests that most sustainable progress is incremental in nature, based on improving existing systems and methods rather than tearing them down and starting from scratch. Wise leaders can recognize opportunities for incremental improvement as well as moments when breakout transformation is possible—which means the Big Hairy Audacious Goals they occasionally embrace are credible and therefore truly inspiring.

Be Funny, Naturally

 HUMOR CAN BE A POWERFUL tool when making a speech, but *how* you use it can make all the difference. The old formula of reciting a stock joke to start your speech often falls flat, especially when the effort at humor is only marginally relevant (as is often the case). Far better is making a spontaneously funny remark that arises naturally from the context of your speech, or even from an audience member's question. With a bit of practice, you'll soon learn whether or not you have the gift of helping people relax with a touch of humor—and if you do, you should take full advantage of it.

Be There for Those Who've Been There for You

 KEEP TRACK OF THE PEOPLE who support you tangibly, materially, and emotionally during your low points in life. They are among your truest friends. These are the people whose faults and mistakes you should be quickest to forgive, and the people whom you should do your utmost to help when *they* are at their own low points. Don't worry too much about *how* to support them. You'll figure it out at the time. Even if you behave awkwardly, being in solidarity with them in time of trouble—when so many people just go missing—is something they will cherish.

Benefit Creep, Be Wary of

 NONPROFITS FACE THE perennial problem of competing for talent with for-profit companies that are usually better-funded and therefore more financially attractive to employees. One common competitive ploy is for the nonprofit to claim that, while its salaries may not be competitive with those in the private sector, their benefit offerings are better. This kind of trade-off may work for a while—but, over time, it can lead to out-of-control benefits packages that are even more expensive than high salaries and even more difficult to rein in. The moral: Expand your benefits package slowly and regularly benchmark it against other employers of all types, thereby avoiding getting too far ahead of the pack.

Big Ears—What They Are and How to Use Them

 I FIRST HEARD THE TERM *big ears* from a musician named Dann Sherrill who was trying to learn a song on the fly while playing it for the first time. In the context of mission-driven leadership, "putting on your big ears" means listening deeply to what people are saying, including the messages they want to communicate but that they are somehow unwilling or unable to say explicitly. This is an important practice in all meetings, but especially in cultivation sessions with donors whom you will later be asking for money. Use your big ears to discern what they may be signaling about their philanthropic preferences—and behave in a way that shows that you have heard and understood their meaning.

Board Management, Studying

THE DEVELOPMENT, CARE, feeding, and management of a high-performing nonprofit board is a complex topic that is the subject of an extensive literature. Most CEOs devote too little time to this activity. As a nonprofit leader, you should devote some time to keeping up with the latest thinking in the field. Read and periodically reread the best books and articles about good practices in board management. Even if you don't agree on every point, your reading will help you think through how to get the most out of your board. One recommendation to start your education: *Governance as Leadership: Reframing the Work of Nonprofit Boards* by Richard P. Chait, William P. Ryan, and Barbara E. Taylor (Wiley, 2004), which I think is the single best book on the subject.

Board Member, How to Be a Good

 ONE WAY TO DEVELOP yourself as a CEO or prepare to become one is to serve on the board of another nonprofit organization. But don't treat board membership as merely a matter of having your ticket stamped or checking off a resume-building box. Resolve to be an active contributor of ideas, experience, energy, connections, money, and other resources. If you find yourself on a dysfunctional board—either one that micromanages staff or simply rubber-stamps their decisions—you have two choices. One is to resign before you frustrate yourself or tarnish your reputation. The other is to try to reform the board, which will take allies, patience, and sometimes the willingness to be highly unpopular. But those are the only two viable options—so choose one. And if you choose to be a reformer, stick with it for a while, and distill as many learnings as you

can from the experience, whether or not
your effort is completely successful.

Body Language, Controlling Your

 WHEN GIVING A SPEECH, remember that the ways you move and your facial expressions may communicate almost as much as your words. Avoid distracting your audience by doing things like fidgeting, shifting your weight from foot to foot, or needlessly adjusting the microphone. Instead, consciously develop a few signature gestures that reinforce particular types of speaking points, and use them in ways that are disciplined but comfortable for you. You may need to study a couple of video clips of yourself in order to recognize the strengths and weaknesses of your body language.

Bonds Between Board and Staff, Building

 IN TOO MANY NONPROFIT organizations, staff members find the board and its functions mysterious and even slightly scary. One way to start breaking down this disconnect is to invite your senior staff to make occasional presentations during board meetings. Also allow those staff members and others from your team to listen in on board meetings, with the exception of executive sessions where highly confidential matters are discussed. Practices like these will help demystify the board and its role in the organization among your staff team, break down silos, and create a sense a camaraderie and transparency. Both your board members and your staff members will learn, grow, and become more energized and committed as a result.

Breaks in Meetings: Using Them Effectively

 WHEN YOU'RE RUNNING a lengthy meeting, schedule a break every 90 minutes or two hours at most. Otherwise you will find attendees losing focus and becoming irritable. As facilitator, use your breaks strategically. In addition to any needed bio break and a brief rest to replenish yourself emotionally, take time to check in with attendees you may be worried about ("You looked uneasy during that last exchange— did you get a chance to fully express your feelings on it?"), to get advice from people whose judgment you trust, and perhaps to get a quick reaction from a few people to an issue or question that has arisen during the meeting. When the scheduled break time is over, enlist attendees to help you round up the others. If need be, just re-start the meeting even if the room is half full—your attendees will stick more rigorously to the scheduled break time in the future.

Call Back Quickly— Especially When You Don't Want To

 BE QUICK ABOUT RETURNING calls from your top contacts—board members, major donors, and other influential stakeholders. Remember that most wealthy, powerful people expect to have their calls returned promptly; even people of more modest means who are heavily invested in your organization probably have the same expectation. Call back quickly even when you feel reluctant to do so. In fact, it's especially important to return calls promptly when you are nervous that the conversation might be difficult to navigate. Since most people put those calls off, you distinguish yourself positively by doing the opposite—and because you avoid letting days pass while your anxiety festers, you help to ensure that the call will probably go better than you fear.

Celebrate Donor Complaints

 QUIETLY CELEBRATE ANY complaint that a donor or prospective donor brings to you about your staff, your board, your organization, or you. Complaints from donors are positive. They show that the donor trusts you to receive the complaint in a mature and professional way and then deal with the situation. Since no organization is perfect—not even yours!—the only alternative is much worse: that your donors remain silent about their complaints, which generates resentment that will drive them away from your mission. So rather than being defensive when a donor offers a complaint, thank them for weighing in, address the issue as best you can, and let the donor know what you've done—thus ensuring that the positive event of receiving a complaint remains positive.

Check the Seat Pocket One More Time

 WHEN TRAVELING, CHECK the seat pocket and the space under your seat at least one extra time beyond what you think necessary before you leave the plane, train, bus, or taxi. Practice the same kind of slightly excessive scrutiny before you check out of your hotel room: Look for your stuff in all the normal places as well as the abnormal ones, like inside the shower, under the bed, and in the dark back corner of the closet shelf. There will be times when being mildly compulsive about this will prevent you from losing something valuable—a phone, a laptop, your toiletry kit, or an irreplaceable file of business papers.

Chronology, Playing with

 EVERY GOOD SPEAKER knows that telling stories is one of the keys to connecting with an audience. And one handy way to make your stories more effective is to play with chronology— that is, the sequence of events. Rather than telling a story straight, in the same order the events happened, you may want to start in midstream to capture your audience's interest and arouse curiosity. You may want to reveal crucial background details sometime in the middle of the narrative to provoke an "Oh, I see!" response. Or you may want to save a particular fact to finish your story with because it is particularly resonant with your core message. Experiment with story-telling sequences until you find one that generates the ideal flow of insight and emotion on the part of your audience.

Chummy, Don't Get Too

 IT'S GREAT TO CULTIVATE relationships with people in adjacent fields who can help or hinder your organization—business leaders, media personalities, politicians, academic experts, and so on. But don't get so chummy that you become reluctant to publicly challenge them if that is what your mission calls you to do. As a leader, accept the truth that there are no *permanent* alliances that should be allowed to take precedence over your continual clear-eyed reevaluation of the best interests of your organization.

Clock, Keep an Eye on the

WHEN RUNNING A MEETING, be a fairly militant timekeeper most of the time. It's the only way to ensure that items near the end of your agenda get covered at all. To do this effectively, tell people in advance that you will be strict about time limits, but inoculate yourself against accusations of being too controlling by inviting them to speak up if they feel you are squelching discussion of an important topic. When you want to move on from an agenda item, ask for the group's permission, but don't wait too long for anyone to object. And always remember that sticking to the schedule, while important, is not as important as getting the big things done for the good of the organization [see Agendas Are Made to Be Bent].

Coalition-Building: Challenging, Frustrating, Essential

 WORKING IN A COALITION with other organizations dedicated to the same mission or to a mission that complements yours is likely to be time-consuming and sometimes frustrating. You'll need to invest energy and hours spent with the leaders of your partner organizations in learning to speak the same language, finding the places where your goals overlap, and dividing roles, responsibilities, and authority fairly. But a well-run coalition can sometimes produce changes that no single organization could ever accomplish alone. And it can create ancillary benefits. For example, the trust you may build with a peer organization may create later opportunities to get advice about a thorny problem, a candid personnel reference or recommendation, and other forms of cooperation.

Comment, Offer a

 WHEN SOMEONE YOU KNOW (or want to know) publishes something, take the time to read or at least skim it, and then offer a supportive comment, either privately or publicly. Nowadays, this is easier than ever thanks to social media. Don't assume the writer won't care. They will, because the number-one motivating factor for anyone who publishes something is not money, fame, or prestige—it's the simple desire to be heard and understood, and to influence how other people think and act.

Compromise, Be Wary of

 IF A CONFLICT BETWEEN two groups or people in your organization reaches the point where it is seriously impacting your mission, try to mediate and find a solution that works for all. But if that proves to be impossible, it's usually best to side with one or the other, even if that means you may have to part ways with someone or an entire group. Splitting the difference will likely make both parties unhappy, leading to continued dissatisfaction and perhaps wholesale defections. Furthermore, if you get into the habit of seeking middle ground somewhere between two clashing views, you encourage people to take extreme positions in an effort to "pull" the final compromise closer to their side. By contrast, if people know you are going to choose a clear winner and a clear loser, they're more likely to make an effort to appear reasonable—which may actually make true cooperation possible.

Conduit to a Donor, How (and How Not) to Cultivate a

IF YOU HAVE ACCESS to a relative or close friend of a wealthy individual you'd like to turn into a donor, expect to invest time in cultivating the linking individual. Avoid treating them as simply a personal conduit, in which case your efforts are likely to backfire. Rather, work with them so that *they* become passionate about your cause. If you succeed, they will probably act on their own to bring their wealthy relative or friend into the fold at a time and in a manner that feels comfortable to them.

Confession Wins Friends

REGULARLY SHARE WITH your senior team and your board of directors your worst recent mistakes. Discuss what they cost the organization and what you feel you learned from them. Encourage them to do the same with their direct reports. If you feel comfortable doing so, share your mistakes with a broader group of organizational stakeholders, such as your most important donors. Your honesty may shock them . . . but it will impress them, too. And it will stand you in good stead on other occasions when you need them to trust your word implicitly.

Consultants Are Human, Too

 AVOID THE TRAP OF taking out your frustrations on your consultants and vendors. Instead, treat them with the same dignity and respect you would accord to your trusted employees or to other valued stakeholders in your organization. Don't negotiate their rates down to the Nth degree, nickel-and-dime them on expenses, or excessively badger them about the quality of their work. If you treat your consultants and vendors well, most will give you extra effort. As for the ones who charge too much or don't deliver, just don't rehire them the next time you have a job to do.

Conversation with a Donor, Steering the

SOMETIMES BEING A LEADER is about imposing your will in order to get the work done. For example, you may find that a conversation with a donor is drifting far from the intended focus due to irrelevant matters raised by a family member, a staff member, or the donor themselves. When this happens, you need to gently but firmly redirect the conversation. To avoid seeming (or feeling) pushy, try saying, "This is very interesting, but out of respect for your time, I'd like to bring the meeting back to its main topic."

Crisis Communications: Take Nothing for Granted

 IN TIMES OF CRISIS, routine activities and behavior often fly out the window. So make a point of checking and double-checking to make sure that basic matters are being handled appropriately. For example, depending on the nature of the crisis, there may be authorities and stakeholders who need to be notified and involved (government agencies, regulatory groups, board members, donors, partners, and so on). Don't assume that someone else has handled these communication tasks; those who would ordinarily do it may be paralyzed by anxiety or uncertainty. Check to be sure the necessary notifications have been made, and, if not, then make them yourself.

Crisis Management: First Steps

WHEN A CRISIS STRIKES your organization, first take a deep breath. Remember that you probably don't know all the relevant facts about the cause of the problem and the best ways to resolve it—which means you don't want to take any major, irrevocable steps in the short term. But you do want to start acting quickly. This will give you and your team a sense of agency and progress. So identify some small but impactful actions you can take in response to the crisis, including sharing basic information with staff, supporters, and stakeholders, and organizing a crisis team to analyze and tackle the problem. Above all, during the early days of the crisis, make an effort to project what I call *grounded optimism* to the people you lead. In other words, acknowledge the seriousness of what has happened while exuding confidence that your group can and will recover.

Criticism: Invite It with Humor

IT CAN BE HARD FOR "the boss" to get honest feedback on an idea he or she puts forward. When you need others to build on or criticize a new idea you've come up with, try using humor to convey that you will not take offense. Delivered with a smile, a line like, "This might just be my worst idea of the day/week/month/year, but here goes . . . " can help create an atmosphere in which candid discussion is possible.

Critics, Responding to

 EVERYONE HAS CRITICS. Some offer criticism that is fair and constructive, others the reverse. Part of being an effective professional is learning to understand, deal with, and learn from both kinds of critics. So a great interview question to ask prospective staff members is "What do your detractors say about you?" It can be followed up with, "How do you respond to those criticisms?" Encourage interviewees to focus on their relatively informed, thoughtful critics, rather than people who appear to be irrationally prejudiced against them. And by the way, even if you're not preparing for a job interview of your own, you ought to think about how *you* would answer these questions, too!

Cultivating Donors: The Three-Week Rule

ALL TOO OFTEN, EVEN very generous donors may feel ignored or taken for granted. This can make them vulnerable to scaling back their support for your organization or shifting their allegiance to another one of the many other nonprofits that will inevitably approach them. To avoid this, make it a habit to touch base with your top donors every three weeks. Call to share some new piece of information, offer to help them in some way, ask for their advice, or request that they support you and your mission in a manner they might enjoy or find meaningful. Certainly don't let a month pass without letting these key donors know that you are thinking of them and that you consider them important members of your team.

Cure for the Blues

 AS OFTEN AS POSSIBLE, try to do something that will "make someone's day" — anyone's day, from a close friend to a stranger. (A friend of mine named Emalyn Mercer did this constantly and was one of the happiest people I have ever known.) If you yourself are feeling down in the dumps, do this even more frequently. It will probably make a big difference to your mood, not to mention how meaningful it may to be to the recipient of your gesture.

Daily Rhythms, Living with Your

 THROUGH OBSERVATION AND experience, learn about your personal daily rhythms. Then, rather than regarding them judgmentally, set about modifying your life and work activities to fit them as best you can. Figure out whether you are more of a morning person or an evening person, and try to schedule important events accordingly. To the extent possible, fit your travel calendar to your personal pattern of energy gain or loss during the course of a day or a trip. (A good practice for many people is to ensure at least 15 minutes of down time between meetings and calls.) Determine what makes you comfortable when you engage in your most common activities, such as typing, talking on the phone, sitting in meetings, or cooking, and then try to organize your days to provide that comfort. As a leader, you deserve it!

Darlings, Killing Your

 GREAT AUTHORS FROM CHEKOV and Faulkner to Oscar Wilde have been credited with the writing advice, "Kill your darlings." It means: Have the fortitude to delete the weakest and most self-indulgent sentences, paragraphs, or pages of your writing, especially when they are personal favorites of yours. The same wisdom applies to nonprofit leadership. You need to learn to recognize when it's time to pull the plug on a struggling or failed project, initiative, or experiment, especially when it's one that you conceived or championed. Most leaders are all too willing to give such projects "just one more chance." As a result, they wait much too long to admit defeat, draining time, energy, money, morale, and other precious resources from their organization in the process.

Deep Breath, Taking a

 THE FIRST RULE OF CRISIS management is to avoid overreacting. Take a deep breath, and realize that, when something goes wrong, it is rarely as bad as you first imagine it to be. If you learn to pause and reflect before acting in moments of crisis, frustration, and even despair, you'll discover that many problems, even ones that initially look insoluble, resolve themselves if you give them time to work themselves out. Occasionally, they turn out to be blessings in disguise. And even when they end up being as serious as you initially feared, taking time to assess them may allow for valuable ideas and allies to emerge unexpectedly.

Denial, Why You Need to Avoid

ALWAYS REMEMBER THAT there are two and only two kinds of organizations: those that regularly experience self-inflicted wounds and admit it, at least to themselves, and those that regularly experience self-inflicted wounds and *don't* admit it. The second type blames external forces or insists that everything is perfect—in other words, they go into denial. You should give up on the notion that there is a third type that magically avoids ever shooting itself in the foot. Then strive to lead the first kind of organization, rather than the second. When you do something foolish that hurts the organization, use the opportunity for self-reflection and to learn something new that will strengthen your management skills for the future. Those who cling to denial pass up such opportunities and often end up repeating the same mistakes.

Dinner with a Donor: Who Pays?

WHEN HAVING A MEAL with a donor, it is generally best to give them the opportunity to (physically) pick up the bill. If and when they do, quickly offer to pay or share the bill, and if they wave you off, offer to do so again. Once they wave you off the second time, simply thank them and put your wallet away. And what if they don't pick up the bill? Then pick it up yourself and make preparations to pay. If they don't intervene to stop you, go ahead and pay the check—and do it gladly, without any sign of disappointment or resentment. (However, if you get stuck with a big bill unexpectedly, you may reconsider where you meet with the same donor in the future.)

Directions, Giving Yourself

 WHEN LEAVING A HOTEL in an unfamiliar city, take with you something with the hotel name, address, and phone number on it, such as the hotel's business card or a piece of stationery. In a non-English-speaking country, make sure this information is in the local language. It may be a lifesaver if you get lost and have to give directions to a taxi driver or police officer who doesn't speak any language you know.

Discretionary Funds: The 15-Percent Rule

 FOUNDATIONS AND OTHER donors like to earmark their financial gifts to nonprofit organizations for specific purposes—understandably so, since they want to make sure that the money they provide goes to support the particular causes they cherish. But a nonprofit also needs a minimum amount of money that it can spend at its own discretion. Otherwise, it's likely to feel hamstrung in its efforts to experiment, address unexpected problems and opportunities, and create organizational cohesion. My experience suggests the absolute minimum level for these discretionary funds is 15 percent. Go lower than this at your peril.

Diversity on Your Board

IT'S VERY DESIRABLE TO build a board that is diverse, and not just in terms of gender or race (important as those are). Diversity in terms of wealth, talent, background, expertise, personality type, and mindset are also important. If you build a board stocked only with rich people, you risk creating a governing body that is prone to groupthink. Instead, consider aiming for a board where one-third of the members are reasonably wealthy (and willing to put that wealth to work for your mission), while the rest offer resources of other kinds—expertise, connections, prestige, access to media influencers, and so on. Of course, the non-wealthy members should be expected to give and raise as much as they can, and they must refrain from treating the wealthy members as human ATMs. And if the number of wealthy board members starts to dwindle, it can cause those who remain to feel they carry an unreasonable burden and prompt them to head for the exits, too. So maintaining the right balance can be complicated—but it's important.

Document Your Donor Interactions

 GET INTO THE HABIT OF thoroughly documenting what happens in every meeting, phone call, or substantive email exchange with a donor. Summarize what was discussed, but also make an effort to capture "irrelevant" details that may prove to be useful or important. Describe the mood of the meeting, and make notes concerning what you've learned about the donor from small talk, family members dropping in, or the photos and memorabilia on display. Keep this file where you can refer to it in the future, and share it with others in your organization who will have occasion to interact with the same donor. These insights and how you use them can help win your group a favored place among the many recipients of your donor's generosity.

"Donor-Driven": A Simplistic Critique of a Nonprofit Organization

 AN OFTEN-HEARD CRITICISM of nonprofit organizations is that they are "donor-driven." This charge is often leveled with little or no explanation, as if it's obvious that an organization that gives weight to the views of its donors is rudderless. This is a lazy form of critique, because the reality is much more complicated. The fact is that the best organizations work continuously to find the sweet spot between donor priorities and their self-assigned mission. This takes both sophisticated strategic thinking and careful attention in internal and external communication, so that stakeholders understand precisely how a particular project fits your broader goals while also meeting the objectives of one or more donors. It's a balancing act too subtle to be captured in the bludgeoning term "donor-driven." [*Also see* "Opportunistic."]

Donor Meetings: The Four-to-Eight-Hour Rule

 AS A NONPROFIT CEO, your job description includes the phrase "fundraiser in chief." There's no way around this. It means that your organization deserves to have you fully prepared for important meetings with your most committed donors and major prospects. And this means that you should expect to spend from four to eight hours preparing for such a meeting (and that does *not* include the time you'll spend traveling to and from the meeting). If you do less than that, you are effectively winging it, and the relationship—and your organization—are likely to suffer as a result. (Many thanks to the terrific nonprofit fundraising consultant Cedric Richner for first bringing this rule to my attention.)

The Dropout Donor, Staying in Touch with

 OCCASIONALLY, A WEALTHY person who has donated a meaningful amount to your organization simply stops giving. When this happens, don't stop cultivating them unless they explicitly tell you not to [*see* Cultivating Donors: The Three-Week Rule]. Even if they *do* ask you to stop cultivating them, you might simply want to pause for six months, then call or write them in an effort to reengage. This kind of respectful, persistent wooing may lead them to resume their previous giving. But even if that doesn't happen, being attentive to them may help ensure that they talk positively about your organization to other philanthropists, which can produce results that are tremendously valuable.

The Dysfunctional Nonprofit Board

 WHEN IT COMES TO THE role of the board in leading a nonprofit organization, the beginning of wisdom is to realize the sad fact that *most nonprofit boards are either entirely or somewhat dysfunctional.* There are surveys that back this up, including one by the Urban Institute in 2012 that spanned more than two thousand organizations. But don't rely on statistics: If you ask people who have served on boards or as senior staff of nonprofits, you will hear quick confirmation of this sad state of affairs. What to do about it? That depends on the nature of the dysfunction. But you won't get anywhere until you start by accepting the reality that your board is probably not operating at its full capacity. And rather than feeling guilty or depressed about it, realize that this is the normal state of affairs, and that if you can build a board that *really works*, you will be well ahead of

the game. But turning around a dysfunctional or mediocre board will take a lot of time and effort; mark your calendar three to five years (not months) in the future, since you will see the full results of your efforts only then.

Encourage the Nervous Speaker

 HAVE YOU EVER BEEN in the audience for a speech or presentation by someone who is obviously very nervous? It's painful to watch, isn't it? When this happens, you don't have to be entirely passive. As soon as the speaker says something that touches or intrigues you, start clapping. Most likely, others will follow suit. This gesture of support will probably help to relax the speaker and enable them to do their best for the rest of the speech—which will make it more enjoyable for you and the rest of the audience. And, by the way, I know this works, because I've had it done for me when I was the nervous speaker.

Ending Your Speech

 WHEN YOU GIVE A SPEECH, you are sometimes asked to conclude by introducing the next speaker or playing some other ceremonial or bridging role. If so, first make sure to formally end your speech, usually by thanking people for their interest and attention, and then stop speaking. This gives the audience a chance to applaud and express their appreciation to you, which gives everyone (including you) a sense of completion about your main remarks. When the applause dies down, you can then perform your ceremonial role.

Enemies, It's Okay to Have a Few

 WHEN YOU ARE NOT OVERLY cautious but instead take some risks in your personal and professional relationships, make peace with the fact that some of those relationships will suffer. Rather than striving to make all your relationships positive all the time, be satisfied if a significantly greater number of people are highly pleased with how you've treated them compared to the number who are disappointed or angry. If you make it your highest priority to avoid ever upsetting or offending anyone, it's likely to make you too cautious, rob you of your spontaneity, and push you toward making safe choices that may not be the most powerful, creative, and forward-looking choices for you or your organization.

Engagement Is Valuable . . . Up to a Point

 INVOLVING TEAMMATES, BOARD members, and outside advisors when tackling a big, important project—for example, defining your organization's multi-year strategy—is both an art and a science. As the leader, it's dangerous for you to control the process too tightly. But it's even more dangerous to outsource it to the point where seemingly endless rounds of "input-gathering" and "reevaluation" threaten to water it down or delay it indefinitely. When you sense that happening, it's time for you to step in and pilot the ship into port. Yes, a few naysayers may complain that they felt "locked out" at the end. But the energy and momentum generated by bringing the project to a successful completion will outweigh their negativity. (I share a detailed case study of how to do this in chapter 10 of my book *Changing the World Without Losing Your Mind*.)

Envy: The Misguided Emotion

 IT'S A COMMON TENDENCY, especially in our celebrity-conscious society, to feel pangs of jealousy with regard to people who are wealthier or more famous than you. Those of us in the nonprofit sector may experience our own unique forms of envy—for example, getting angry over the fact that our work is devalued in comparison to that of pop singers or TV personalities whose contribution to society is, at best, questionable. When thoughts like this start to irk you, reflect on the advantages of *not* being a wealthy celebrity. You can walk around without being harassed by fans or the paparazzi; you'll never be assailed by thousands of strangers for a stray remark on Twitter; and you'll never have to wonder whether your friends like you for yourself rather than for your wealth or fame. So in addition to being a waste of energy, envy is also mostly downright dumb.

Exercise, Making Time to

 WHEN TRAVELING FOR WORK, it's easy to get out of the exercise habit—yet this is one of the times when you need it most. The long hours, time zone changes, ceremonial meals, intense meetings, and other demands of travel can be stressful and exhausting. Working out can be a great way to relieve stress. So find ways to build in daily physical exercise when you are on the road, even if this means sacrificing a bit of quality or preparation for your meetings and projects or cutting your sleep short by an hour. If going to the gym or for a run is impractical, at least make time to simply walk up a flight or two of stairs rather than taking the elevator.

Fair-Weather Friend, Be More Than a

IF YOU BENEFITED FROM an experience, a job, or a personal relationship, say so honestly when you are part of a group sharing stories about their lives—and do so whether or not the people or organizations involved are currently considered prestigious or popular. Don't disown or disavow someone or something that you grew from, even if embracing them may embarrass you in some way. Your roots are your roots, and it's unseemly to be ashamed of them.

The Family Liaison—Follow Your Donors' Lead

 WHEN A WEALTHY FAMILY supports a nonprofit organization, it usually designates one family member or staff member to serve as a liaison with the organization. If you are working with such a donor family, follow their lead. Work exclusively with the designated liaison until they direct you to do otherwise. It is almost never appropriate or helpful to go around your designated point of contact to try to get additional funding or support from other family members, so resist any temptation to do so.

Feedback Sandwich, The Art of the

WHEN SOMEONE ASKS FOR your feedback—on their work, their leadership style, a speech or a paper they've prepared, or anything else— take it as a compliment, and provide the feedback as best you can. A good practice is to offer a feedback sandwich: a layer of critical commentary between two slices of praise. Starting on a positive note will likely relax the person and allow them to take on board the rest of your feedback, while ending with a compliment will help them walk away feeling encouraged and energized rather than downcast.

Friendship Is More Than a Transaction

 YOU CAN ENRICH YOUR LIFE by making the time to keep in regular touch with a dozen or so of your best friends. Check in with them every few weeks and, if you live in different parts of the country, make a point to see them when you happen to be in the same city. Some may reciprocate. But don't *expect* them to do so, and don't make reciprocation a condition of your friendship. Other people may have complexities in their lives that you don't understand, appreciate, or share. So as long as it gives you pleasure to make time for these people, do so, regardless of whether they respond in precisely equal fashion.

From "Either/Or" to "Both/And"

 IF YOU ARE STRUGGLING WITH a problem that seems to require a painful and unsatisfying choice between two alternatives—in particular, two good outcomes that you find equally attractive and important—try calling in your most trusted friends and advisors to talk you through the conundrum. Those with a fresh perspective may be able to help you see beyond a false dichotomy in which you feel trapped. There may well be a creative "both/and" option that you'll be able to envision once you escape the limitations of "either/or."

Fundraise Like You Mean It

 WHEN IT COMES TO FUNDRAISING, have the courage of your convictions. Never, ever ask for money apologetically or hesitantly. You are passionate about your organization and its mission—show it! Excitement can be contagious. Remember that it could very well be that the invitation to support your cause will be as thrilling to the donor as it is to you, if not more so. And don't be discouraged if your prospective donor doesn't immediately show signs of having caught your enthusiasm. We all show our feelings differently, and the contagious power of your message may only become clear when you receive a check in the mail.

Fundraising Improv, The Art of

IN FUNDRAISING AS IN LIFE, meticulous preparation is one key to success. Have a clear, well-thought-out plan for any important meeting, call, or event with a major donor or potential donor. But also be prepared for the unexpected. When something you didn't anticipate happens, don't play it safe by sticking to your script or withdrawing from the encounter. Instead, be willing to think on your feet and improvise. Remember that, in moments like these, being imperfect in the service of your mission is far better than disappearing (literally or figuratively) due to fear of imperfection. (*Also see* The Jackpot Question, Being Prepared for.)

Fundraising Talent, Finding and Nurturing

 IN THE NONPROFIT WORLD, fundraising talent is a rare and highly valued commodity. If you lead a mission-driven organization, you'll discover just how hard it is to find and retain truly gifted fundraisers. Some third-rate fundraisers have learned how to pass themselves off as first-rate through their finely tuned interviewing skills. If you accidentally hire one of these pretenders, your only choice is to cut your losses once you discover your mistake. On the other hand, when you find—or better yet, grow from within your organization—a really good fundraising talent, hold on to them for as long as you can, even if they have flaws or quirks. As long as they are ethical, hard-working, willing to learn, and loyal to the organization and its mission, they are worth keeping and investing in.

The Gala Dinner: Annual May Not Be Best

 THE TRADITIONAL GALA DINNER is generally a fairly inefficient way to generate revenue, and it's easy to become too reliant on. But the gala has its place in a comprehensive fundraising program. Consider holding one every three to five years, which can be a good compromise between an annual gala and no gala at all. And when you do plan a big event, call on the help of experienced event planners, production companies, charity auctioneers, and the like. A gala planned and staged by amateurs can be a costly and unproductive waste of time and energy and diminish your public standing.

Generosity to Others: The 30-Minute Rule

 WHEN SOMEONE ASKS YOU for a favor—a friend of a friend, an acquaintance, a professional peer, or even a stranger—consider using the 30-minute rule to decide whether or not you'll grant the request: If the task will take you 30 minutes or less, go for it. If you eventually find that you've become so busy helping other people that your own work is being neglected, lower the threshold to 10 or 20 minutes. Whatever level you choose, follow the rule, and get into the habit of automatically saying yes to any request that meets the requirement. I predict you'll find that the universe repays you for your reflexive generosity many times over.

The Get-Out-of-Jail-Free Card

 IN YOUR RELATIONSHIPS WITH staff, colleagues, supporters, and friends, give everyone an annual get-out-of-jail-free card. In other words, offer them free and complete forgiveness for a mistake they make in the way they behave toward you . . . the first time. But if they repeat the same mistake a second and a third time, you'll probably decide not to make the card available again, especially for that particular kind of transgression.

"Giving at the Office": Why It's Not Enough

 EVERYONE SHOULD LOOK FOR opportunities to make society better as they go about their daily lives. This is especially important for those of us who lead mission-driven organizations. There needs to be a high level of consistency between our professional behavior and goals and the way we conduct ourselves when we're not on the job. If contributing to society even in very small ways is something you do only "at the office," people are likely to sense a lack of coherence in your behavior and values. Once this happens, it can raise questions about your ethics, character, and motivations, and even cast doubt on the causes to which you've dedicated your career.

Going Green

 DO ALL YOU CAN TO STRUCTURE your life and your organizational processes in ways that reduce your environmental footprint and resource consumption. (Thankfully, new options to achieve this become available with every passing year.) But don't become obsessed with going green or beat yourself up for those things you find too challenging to reduce or eliminate. Falling into unproductive self-recriminations does no one any good, and neither does giving up on sustainability altogether due to despair over its difficulty. Instead, combine your (inevitably modest) personal efforts with support for organizations that advocate for public-policy reform and society-wide programs to conserve more and pollute less.

Good Is Often Good Enough

 IN SOME ASPECTS OF management and leadership, perfectionism is unnecessary and may even be unhealthy. The search for perfection—the perfect technique, the perfect mood for the job, or the perfect comment—can lead you to procrastinate rather than acting immediately, while the issue is fresh in your mind. Common examples include writing and mailing thank-you notes, praising people who've earned it, and preparing written and oral reports to your stakeholders. The crucial skill you need to continually practice is accurately distinguishing the relatively few most-important tasks that demand the highest standard of excellence from the many tasks for which timeliness and efficiency are more significant than getting it *just right*. If you insist on near-perfection in all your tasks, sooner or later you'll burn yourself and your team out.

Grassroots, Feeding at the

EARLY IN YOUR NONPROFIT career, you may not make much money or enjoy many perks. But one benefit you may have is the opportunity to spend time at the grassroots level where the social problem you are trying to address is most visible and tangible. Treasure those moments and extract from them as much insight and understanding as possible. As your career advances, you may not have many more opportunities like that, so take full advantage of the opportunities you do get, even if your energy is low or you are stressed. Deep knowledge of the conditions experienced by that those you want to serve, whether gained from past exposure or more recent immersion, however limited, will make you a more credible and effective decision-maker, spokesperson, and leader.

Grateful Traveler, Being a

 PEOPLE IN THE TRANSPORTATION and hospitality industries usually work hard, often without the appreciation and rewards they deserve. When they serve you well, thank them, and tip them at least as well as local custom dictates. Don't forget to tip the staff that clean and service your hotel room. It's best to leave a small daily tip for them rather than giving one large tip at the end of your stay, since the staff members rotate in and out from day to day. You may also want to put your tips for the housecleaning staff somewhat out of view so that when supervisors come to check your fridge or mini bar, they won't be able to easily take gratuities meant for others. I'm convinced that, if you are a consistently generous traveler, the travel gods will reward you.

Habits, Keeping Track of Your Roster of

 NO ONE HAS ONLY HEALTHY habits. So don't be too harsh on yourself if you have a couple of unhealthy ones—a love of fried foods, a tendency to put off visiting the doctor. Instead, just try to have more healthy habits than unhealthy ones. Especially if you sense your personal balance of healthy/unhealthy habits is out of kilter, attempt to add at least one new healthy habit per year, or break one unhealthy habit.

Hang Out, Letting It All

AS A LEADER, YOU'LL BE tempted to become cautious regarding what you say and write on behalf of your organization. You'll express your emotions with care and avoid sounding extreme in any way. This is generally a good thing. But consider occasionally throwing caution to the wind. Look for a time and place when speaking with candor and intense feeling will be appropriate and even necessary. Your audience will be surprised; some may think you've gone too far. But you may win the admiration and loyalty of many others who share the feelings you've expressed and emerge from the experience with a deeper sense of empathy for and loyalty to you.

Have Fear—Don't Let It Have You

 FEAR IS AN INEVITABLE PART of the human condition. You *will* experience it from time to time, *especially* if you are a first-time nonprofit leader. Sometimes it's associated with activities that are genuinely dangerous (taking a big financial risk), other times with activities that are actually quite safe and potentially even beneficial (giving a speech, meeting new people, traveling to an unfamiliar country). Since fear can never be completely eliminated from our lives, consciously train yourself to simply *have* fear rather than letting fear *have you*—that is, control you. One way to achieve this is to push yourself to do more of the things that frighten you (the safe kind), and to enjoy the sense of accomplishment and pride you feel whenever you hold fear at bay enough to push through.

Helping, Saying Yes to

 EACH DAY, TRY TO SAY yes to at least one request to help someone that you are initially not inclined to grant. Each day, also try to say yes to at least one offer of help that you are initially not inclined to accept. You'll be doing your part to move us toward a world in which more and more people are biased toward helping one another in ways large and small—which is the kind of world most of us would like to live in.

Hobbies as Icebreakers

 WHILE WAITING FOR A business meeting to start, turn to someone nearby and ask them about their hobbies. In exchange, share your own. Not only is this a more interesting alternative than the usual small-talk topics (the weather, local sports, when did you arrive in town, and so on), it can also lead to refreshing opportunities when you're on a business trip. Your new acquaintance may offer a suggestion about how you can indulge your own hobbies in their city, and if you happen to share a hobby with them (such as biking, gallery-hopping, or listening to live jazz), they may invite you to join them for something fun—which will make your trip more enjoyable and help you deepen a professional relationship at the same time.

Home Field Advantage, Yielding the

WHEN DEALING WITH A thorny, emotional problem—a dispute with a colleague, for instance—it's usually best to try to discuss the most difficult issues in person, using a facilitator if appropriate. (An exception may arise if you're dealing with someone for whom communicating in writing is much less stressful.) The location for the meeting can be important. Look for a neutral place, or, even better, offer to use a setting in which your antagonist is likely to be most comfortable—for example, in their own office rather than in yours. This kind of small, gracious gesture can pave the way to a more open and constructive conversation.

Hotel Room Security

 WHILE TRAVELING FOR WORK, when you leave your hotel for a meal or a meeting, bring with you only the devices, credit cards, cash, and identification you will need. Leave your other valuables locked up in your suitcase, where they will likely be safer than in your coat pocket or purse, or sitting out on a desk or table in your hotel room.

Idea Bubble, Breaking Out of the

 NOWADAYS IT IS EASIER than ever to spend all our time immersed in bubbles or echo-chambers where we are exposed only to ideas, information, stories, and experiences that reinforce what we already believe. It's a natural human tendency to want to stay inside this bubble—after all, it's comfortable and pleasant to have your pre-existing biases continually reinforced. Make a deliberate effort to break this pattern. Spend some time every week reading or otherwise exploring things that challenge your political ideology, your religious faith (or lack thereof), and your most cherished values. You may learn some things that will lead you to challenge your own complacency. But even if you don't, you will almost surely gain a deeper and more nuanced understanding of *why* you believe what you do, and a stronger ability to explain those beliefs to others.

Ignorance: Remembering It When You Negotiate

 DURING NEGOTIATIONS WITH internal or external stakeholders or partners, always remember that there are significant unknown factors that will impact the outcome. For example, you can never fully know the motivations, goals, fears, and needs of the people on the other side of the table, nor can you be completely sure of any alternative options they may have. As a result, it's easy to significantly overestimate or underestimate the strength of your own position. Instead, try to keep an even keel, and look continuously for previously unrecognized leverage (on their part or yours) and the potential for unusual win-win solutions. And be ready for last-minute snafus that short-circuit what felt like a completed negotiation. When they arise, don't lose your equanimity, but rather stay focused on getting back on track to closure.

"I'll Have the Cobb Salad . . . and a Generous Donation"

 FOR MOST PEOPLE, fundraising is a combination of intuitive and counter-intuitive elements. One counter-intuitive lesson that works for me is to get "the ask"—including the specific dollar amount—out on the table early in your meeting with a donor: during the first five minutes if possible, or at least during the first third of the meeting. So, for example, if the meeting is over a meal at a restaurant, make the ask within five minutes of placing your orders. (Typically, the time before orders are taken is best spent on ice-breaking small talk.) This may take a bit of courage on your part, but it allows the rest of your conversation to deal directly and constructively with the issue that you both know is the purpose of the meeting, rather than relegating it to a few minutes at the end, or, worse yet, leaving the request vague or unspoken.

Important but Not Urgent

 IN OUR FRANTIC LIVES, the urgent often drives out the important. In the long run, we and our organizations suffer as a result. To combat this tendency, carve out some time every month to do things that are important but not urgent. Examples: backing up your computer files, going for your annual physical, calling a relative or old friend you haven't talked to in a while, storing your most valuable documents in a fireproof safe, cooking your significant other a really nice meal, planning your escape from your home during a fire, or taking a colleague or a young person who looks up to you out for his or her favorite lunch.

Interview, Preparing for an

IF YOU OR YOUR ORGANIZATION achieve some degree of fame, you may find yourself being asked to participate in an interview on radio, television, or before a live audience (that is, a "fireside chat" with a moderator). Congratulations! You'll probably feel very excited about the opportunity. But don't prepare by doing what your instincts may suggest—that is, by trying to predict the questions you'll be asked and then to write and rehearse the perfect responses to them. Having lived through this experience more than once, I can tell you what's likely to happen: The interviewer is almost certain to ask you questions you never anticipated, or to raise familiar topics in unfamiliar contexts and using unfamiliar terms. Your canned answers are then likely to sound robotic or be useless to you, leaving you flummoxed. So rather than listing questions and prepared answers, just list the handful of core messages you'd like to convey. Then approach the interview as a true conversation, remaining open-minded to the give and take of ideas and ready to go with the flow. The result will be more enjoyable for you as well as your audience—and the real you will have a much better chance to shine.

The Introduction—Getting It Right

 WHEN YOU'RE SCHEDULED to give a speech, connect in advance with the person who will be introducing you to make sure they hit the right notes. If you are representing your organization (and especially if it is not already well known to all of those in attendance), make sure the person introducing you includes a concise one- to two-minute summary of what the organization does (or, if they fail to do so, then do it yourself at the beginning of your remarks). Equally important, make sure it does *not* include extraneous facts like a long list of the boards you serve on or the journals in which your articles have been published. You don't want your audience to be half asleep before you even begin your speech, do you?

Invitations, Think Twice About

WHEN ANYONE ASKS OR invites you to some event—whether they are family, friend, colleague, acquaintance, or stranger—resist the urge to immediately say no. Instead, take a moment to think about what you might gain from saying yes, including the likelihood that you will make the day of the person inviting you (and perhaps prompt them to make *your* day at some point in the future). Look for an opportunity at least once a week to accept an invitation you initially planned to decline—and this applies to you *especially* if you are in the habit of thinking of your life as "much too busy." You have probably been unwittingly foreclosing some easy opportunities to learn, grow, and deepen your personal and professional relationships.

The Jackpot Question, Being Prepared for

 WHILE SOME MEETINGS with potential donors — especially first meetings — are not well suited to making a direct solicitation for financial support, you can never be sure what may happen once the conversation begins. For this reason, it's important to always be prepared with a good answer for the possible jackpot question: "What could your organization do if I wrote you a check for $1 million today?" If you can respond to the jackpot question clearly and without appearing flustered, you just may increase the odds of having the dream come true! On the other hand, if you can't answer such a question cogently, you may need to spend some time reflecting . . . or maybe even find another line of work.

Join the Debate

 EVERY PROFESSIONAL FIELD has its ongoing debates. A strong leader is willing to publicly participate in at least some of those debates. This can be especially valuable if you happen to have well-thought-out, fact-based opinions that are not shared by a majority of your peers at other organizations. Your contrarian views, clearly articulated and energetically defended, may become a point of differentiation and pride among your colleagues, helping to mark you and your organization as among the thought leaders in your field. And you will have a deep sense of satisfaction when some of your minority and unpopular views later become widely accepted.

Joking Matter, The Painful Past Is Not a

 GETTING OVER A PAINFUL EPISODE from the past can be tricky, in an organizational context just as in a family or social context. When a colleague or associate has done you wrong, lied to you, or otherwise let you down, avoid reminding them of their transgression, especially if they have made amends. This includes making supposedly humorous references to the past incident. Not only is this kind of joking hurtful, it may serve as a self-fulfilling prophesy that contributes to a negative pattern repeating itself.

Joy, Taking Time for

 FIGURE OUT WHICH ACTIVITIES in life reduce your stress level and bring you joy. This may take a bit of experimentation: Try new and unfamiliar activities from time to time, and when you find one that seems to work for you, embrace it. These activities can range from small things—like getting your shoes shined or your nails done—to bigger things, like skiing or setting aside a day to spend in a place you love. For me, listening to live music in an intimate venue is an activity that reliably helps me to relax and re-engage with life. Once you've found the activities that kindle your sense of joy, invest the time and money needed to make them a regular part of your life. They'll pay dividends in the form of increased energy, creativity, and productivity.

Kryptonite Against an "Unfair Dismissal" Lawsuit

 . . . IS TO FIRE PEOPLE IN A WAY that respects their dignity and treats them fairly. That means having an honest reason why their firing is unavoidable, explaining it truthfully and empathetically, and giving them both a fair severance package and (if they desire it) outplacement assistance. If you follow these principles religiously, not only will your former team members forego legal action but it's likely they'll even speak well of your organization in the future once they get over the pain of having been let go.

Language, Learning a New

 EVERY TEN TO FIFTEEN YEARS, try to learn a new language. In between these periods, find ways to practice the languages you previously learned, so that your knowledge stays reasonably fresh. This can be challenging, even scary to do, because using a language other than your native tongue requires you to face and master your fear of looking foolish. That's a valuable habit in and of itself.

Laughter, Healthy and Unhealthy

 ALWAYS BE READY TO LAUGH at yourself and at the absurdities of life—it's a great antidote to the human tendency to take the moment-by-moment vicissitudes and our own reaction to them with excessive seriousness. But avoid falling into the habit of indulging in unhealthy forms of humor—for example, excessive use of self-deprecating jokes that amount to self-abasement, or the use of sarcasm and mockery as a way of expressing hostility in a deniable form.

Leave the Nest, Letting Your Babies

WHEN YOU OR YOUR TEAM have conceived and successfully launched a program, a project, or an innovative idea, it's natural to feel excited and proud—which can lead to a permanent sense of attachment. Yet sometimes an organization is meant to be an incubator for something new rather than its permanent home. When an initiative you've created gets too big or complex to be comfortably housed under your roof . . . when it begins taking so much of your time and energy that your other projects are being neglected . . . or when it naturally starts to evolve in a direction that doesn't really fit the mission of your organization—then it's time for you to recognize that the baby is ready to leave the nest and move out on its own. Accept this bittersweet realization with the pride you've earned!

Letter, The Magic of a

 WHENEVER YOU CAN, WRITE old-fashioned letters to your donors, volunteers, and colleagues to tell them what you appreciate most about them. The letter could be motivated by a milestone in the recipient's life, a notable accomplishment, a special act of kindness, or nothing in particular. A handwritten note is very effective; so is a typed letter spanning two or three single-spaced pages. A letter mailed from an unexpected location, such as an overseas assignment or a favorite vacation spot, stands out even more. A heartfelt personal letter can be one of the most effective ways to communicate to a person you care about that you don't take them for granted. Unlike a spoken expression of appreciation or admiration, it can easily be reread periodically and shared with others.

Life Beyond the Board

 OCCASIONALLY YOU WILL develop a relationship with a talented, energetic person who likes your organization and strikes you as exactly the sort of person you'd like to recruit for your board of directors. Wonderful! But if, upon probing, you discover that they *don't* want to serve on your board, don't be too downhearted. Work with them to co-create one or more customized ways for them to serve your mission that suit their engagement preferences. Perhaps they'd like to serve as an ambassador, spreading the good word about your work [*see* Ambassadors for Your Organization—How to Manage Them]. Perhaps they'd like to serve as formal or informal advisors, members of a specifically tailored committee, or the guiding lights behind a new initiative they'll help conceive and design. The possibilities are limited only by their talents and your imagination.

Lifelong Learning (1)

 I FIRST HEARD THE TERM "lifelong learner" from David Lawrence, the Florida-based children's advocate who previously was the publisher of the *Miami Herald*. One day, David invited a colleague and me to meet him in a diner. We found him sitting in a booth, reading a book. He told us that he read one book per week, and had done so for decades. I was surprised, having assumed, I suppose, that at some point a person like him would decide he'd "learned enough." But David taught me that, once your curiosity diminishes, so does your ability to work, teach, and relate effectively to others.

Lifelong Learning (2)

 NORM TONINA, A MENTOR and former colleague of mine, applied the idea of being a "lifelong learner" in another way. In highly charged personal conflicts, people tend to harden their positions, become self-righteous and indignant, draw conclusions about other people's motivations, and become fixated on a single acceptable resolution. (I have certainly fallen into that trap.) Norm taught me that being a lifelong learner offers a way out. If you are always curious, open to new information, interested in different interpretations of others' behavior, and willing to consider fresh and creative resolutions to problems, conflicts tend to get solved far more easily and peacefully. Like most people, I have found Norm's advice hard to apply at times. But when I have, it has often worked wonders.

Loyalty Isn't the Point

 IF YOU WANT TO BUILD a board of directors whose members are truly critical, independent thinkers—and you should!—then beware of members who reflexively and automatically either defend or criticize the CEO or the staff. Examining your organization's programs, policies, and practices shouldn't be about "loyalty" or "disloyalty," and you shouldn't allow board members to frame the issues in those terms. Instead, encourage them to approach each issue that comes before them with curious, open minds and judge them on the merits—and if any members are incapable of doing so, gently suggest they step down from the board and find another way to contribute. In other words, board members should always be encouraged to speak their minds and vote their consciences. Doing so increases their value to your organization enormously.

Magic Place, Finding Your

BE ON THE LOOKOUT FOR at least one place that allows you to temporarily slip into a different persona and way of living that gives you more joy—or perhaps a different kind of joy—than you normally experience. It may be a physical place, as Key West, Florida, is for me. It may be a metaphorical "place" built around a meaningful activity. For my wife, it is skiing; for others, it may be a meditation retreat or a walk in the woods. Once you identify the place that brings you this special joy, make time to go there regularly. The positive impact on your life and your work will be enormous.

Matching Projects to People

 DON'T THINK OF ASKING PEOPLE to volunteer for your organization as taking their time away from what *they* want and redirecting it to what *you* want. Instead, think of it as giving them a satisfying way to advance their careers and learn new skills while contributing something special to society. To make this happen, keep your eyes out for projects that match the interests and resources of particular board members or volunteers. Then give those individuals the freedom to take some real ownership of their projects (while reserving final decision-making authority on important matters to your staff). This will take burdens off your shoulders, ensure good project results, and produce motivated, satisfied, and loyal volunteers. (You can read about a classic case of this idea in action in chapter 13 of my book *Changing the World Without Losing Your Mind*.)

Meeting, How to Start a

 GOOD MEETINGS USUALLY BEGIN with a mixture of formality (welcoming people), good governance (asking for approval of and any amendments to the written agenda), and, perhaps most important, context setting: Why are we here? What do we hope to accomplish? Spend a few minutes reflecting on the journey that the group is on together, how far you have come, how this meeting relates to the larger mission, and what you need to achieve today. In the course of this conversation, try to tune in to the emotional state of each participant, so you'll be well equipped to steer the meeting in a positive, constructive direction.

Meetings, Encouraging Regular Attendance at

 WHEN YOU LEAD A GROUP that holds periodic meetings, make a point of encouraging members to attend as consistently as possible. Having an ever-changing group of attendees, including regular drops-ins by people not formally part of the group, is not a good recipe for team cohesion and ensuring forward momentum. This also means that you need to lead by example by resisting the urge to change meeting dates or miss a session when something more attractive comes along.

Mentors, Staying in Touch with

 STAY IN TOUCH WITH YOUR past mentors and other people who helped you at various stages of your life. Share with them the highlights of your life journey, and tell them how their assistance continues to shape and benefit you and the people and causes you care about. This may mean tracking someone down to give them a copy of an article or a book you wrote that was in part inspired by them; it may mean something as simple as dashing off a quick email to let someone know that their past words or actions helped you solve a recent problem. Doing so will make them—and you—feel good. It will also remind you of the important truth that we accomplish very little entirely by ourselves.

Messaging Change: The Four-Part System

 THE ESSENCE OF GOOD NONPROFIT leadership is to consistently deliver some version of the following four-part message about change to your staff, your volunteers, your donors, and your other stakeholders. (1) The change we're seeking to make in society is *important.* (2) That change is *possible, but not inevitable.* (3) We have an effective and in some way unique way of making that change. (4) If we work hard, we will be able to take real satisfaction in impacting society for the better, and we'll be recognized for doing so. If you and your whole team internalize this four-part message, there's very little you can't achieve.

Metrics Matter . . . But Keep Them Simple

 SINCE YOUR MISSION-DRIVEN organization likely lacks the familiar measures of success that commercial enterprises have, such as sales, profits, and stock price, be deliberate about building ways to credibly measure the success of your work. Tackle this task as soon as you can, since it's much easier to devise clear, understandable metrics in the early days of a project than after it's underway. But don't obsess about creating metrics that are ultra-detailed and logically ironclad. In this area, as in so many others, avoid making the perfect the enemy of the good. Instead, put a premium on metrics that are simple, easy to calculate, and memorable—and periodically have the results verified and confirmed through rigorous third-party evaluations.

Microphone, Working the

 WHEN GIVING A SPEECH, it's usually best to have your mouth about eight to twelve inches from the microphone. Closer than the optimal distance can lead to distortion, and farther away may make you hard to hear. If you clap while at the podium, hold your hands a good distance from the microphone so that the sound does not become distracting or even deafening to the audience.

Milestone Moments as Occasions for Giving

 THERE ARE CERTAIN TIMES in the life of an organization that tend to loosen donors' purse-strings and make them more prone to outsized generosity—for example, a key start-up event, the launch of a strategic plan, or an important anniversary. In the same way, donors may be more inclined to make large gifts when they experience one of *their own* milestone moments—for example, after recovery from a near-death experience, after the loss of a loved one, or when celebrating a wedding or childbirth. Take advantage of such opportunities with sensitive but aggressive solicitations.

"Mission Accomplished"? Not So Fast!

 WHEN YOU ACHIEVE A meaningful project milestone, it's good to celebrate—but beware of declaring victory too early. Securing money for a project, passing a piece of legislation, or getting a school built may just be an intermediate step in the much bigger process of having a positive impact on society. See the process through before you claim victory too vigorously. Make sure the money is spent wisely, ensure that the new law is implemented effectively, and track the ways the lives of students are improved by the new school— and check back periodically to confirm that the positive impact is sustained over time.

Mistakes, Make the Most of

MANAGING DONOR RELATIONS is an important part of the work of a nonprofit leader. It's not a happy time when a serious mistake is made with a major donor, causing them to be displeased with your organization. But when this happens, it's no time to give up or stick your head in the sand. Rather, use it as an opportunity to distinguish your organization as one that responds to problems in creative, proactive, and pragmatic ways. Connect with the donor, discuss what happened, show empathy for their unhappiness, and figure out together what you can do to remedy the problem. In so doing, you may be able to turn a negative into a positive, making the relationship between the donor and your organization stronger than ever.

Moderator, Being an Effective

WHEN MODERATING A PANEL discussion at a conference, take a strong hand. This doesn't necessarily mean talking a lot. Your main job is to nudge the panelists off their scripted talking points so that they can address the panel's topic in a way that feels spontaneous, interactive, and enlightening. That may require asking provocative questions, interrupting panelists (politely), encouraging them to speak to one another, asking them to offer stories, and otherwise creatively shaking up the process. Author Adam Grant has a blog post on LinkedIn, titled "How to Run a Conference Panel That Isn't Horrible," which offers some fine additional tips.

Money and Joy

 HERE IS A FORMULA FOR drastically reducing the amount of angst you experience over your finances: Spend money liberally and without guilt on a *few* things that bring you joy. Be frugal in all other areas. Then, periodically reevaluate whether the things you have been spending on freely still bring you joy. If they don't, scale back or discontinue spending on those things, and shift your spending to other things that now bring you joy. Living like this will not increase your income—but it's guaranteed to increase the amount of happiness you experience for every dollar in your wallet.

Name Game, Playing the

 PEOPLE CARE ABOUT THEIR names; it matters to them to have other people notice and remember their names. So work on being good about names. Make an effort to remember the names of people who regularly work with you or serve you (in your favorite restaurant, for example), as well as their relatives and close friends. When you meet someone, say their name out loud as soon as possible. Later, write it on your phone or on a scrap of paper. And when you're going to be with someone whose name you have trouble recalling, take a moment to ask someone else to help you remember it.

New Ideas, How to Encourage

REGULAR ONE-ON-ONE MEETINGS with your direct reports and their direct reports are a great way to encourage people to give you their best thinking about how you can lead the organization better. Use these meetings to solicit suggestions and to receive them with openness, appreciation, and curiosity. Don't be too quick to dismiss the ideas you're given, express gratitude if you try them successfully, and don't blame the source if you try them and they fail. This combination of strategies will demonstrate to people that you are serious about wanting fresh ideas, helping to ensure that such ideas will continue to flow your way.

New Leaf: The 3-to-5-Year Rule

 FROM TIME TO TIME, YOU'LL be working with a colleague or partner who has a character trait that doesn't serve them well—habitual dishonesty, a tendency to be scatterbrained, an uncontrolled temper, or the like. The time may come when this person announces that they are turning over a new leaf and intend to change their ways. Of course, you should praise and encourage them in this effort—but don't assume your relationship with them will change significantly any time soon as a result of their promise of a new behavior. In most cases, changing a fundamental character trait takes three to five years. Make any decisions you need to make (about their continued employment in your organization, for example) on the basis of this realistic expectation.

No Excuses

 WE ALL HAVE A BAD DAY from time to time. Don't make excuses for your job performance based on lack of sleep, excessive travel, unreasonable expectations from others, or family responsibilities, unless people clearly want to hear about your problems. They rarely do.

Not Enough Chairs

 WHEN GIVING A SPEECH, or hosting one, remember that a full-looking room inspires most speakers to do their best, while empty chairs, especially in the front row, tend to have the opposite effect. To encourage the speaker and to create the impression that today's talk is a "hot ticket," set out just six chairs for every ten people who RSVP'd (and fewer if the weather is bad). You can always keep a few seats in reserve to be added if more people show up—a ritual that adds a bit of last-minute excitement and anticipation to the event.

The Numbers Game: Play It Straight

IT'S GREAT TO INCLUDE ON your nonprofit board some members from the business, corporate, and government sectors. But this can occasionally lead to needless confusion or mistrust, especially when it comes to finance and accounting, where the rules applied to nonprofits are quite different from those in other sectors. To neutralize this, invite the chief financial officer from a nonprofit larger than yours onto your board. This individual can vouch for your team when they are doing things that may look odd but that are in fact strictly proper according to nonprofit accounting rules.

Nurturing Board Members: The 2x Rule

 SPEND DOUBLE (OR EVEN TRIPLE) the amount of time with your board members than you want to or think you should. Every board meeting, committee meeting, and one-on-one meeting should be well planned, productive, efficient, and as enjoyable as possible. They should also give members a sense of connection to the mission and the feeling of satisfaction that comes from having accomplished something meaningful. Finally, they should be followed up diligently by you and your team to reinforce that the board members' role and input are valued. And during times of organizational growth or crisis, spend even *more* time with your board members. All of the same rules apply to former board members who demonstrate that they want to remain involved.

One-on-One Conversations, The Power of

 DURING MOMENTS OF organizational conflict, change, and risk, the communication techniques you employ as a leader become doubly important. One powerful tool to employ at such times is one-on-one conversations with your core people—the staff members, allies, supporters, and stakeholders who will play crucial roles in helping you successfully navigate the turbulence. Spend time telling them why you are leading the organization the way you are, answer their urgent questions, respond to the concerns and fears they might not be willing to express in a group meeting, and ask for their candid advice. The time you invest in these heart-to-heart talks will generate valuable dividends in the form of improved morale, a shared vision, support for your leadership, and team solidarity.

One Night's Sleep, Surviving the Loss of

TRAVELING FOR WORK can wreak havoc with our sleep schedules. However, if you're like most people, you can sustain a high or at least moderate level of work performance after missing all (or most of) a single night's sleep. To do this, think positively: Don't let yourself freak out because you've missed your accustomed number of hours of shut-eye [see Sleeplessness, Making the Best of]. Then make sure you do whatever you need to do to get some decent rest the following night, so the remainder of your week can be reasonably comfortable and productive.

Open a Space for Outsiders

 WHEN YOU ARE AN ORGANIZATIONAL leader—or when you are one of the more popular, respected, or powerful people in a group, or otherwise have high status—look for opportunities to visibly value and involve those who are less popular, less powerful, or have lower status. Call on them in meetings; invite them to participate in projects; ask for their input when issues are being debated. Your action will send an important signal to everyone, subtly moving the organization toward being more inclusive and democratic. Not incidentally, it will likely elicit some valuable new ideas and perspectives that will benefit everyone.

"Opportunistic": A Simplistic Critique of a Nonprofit Organization

 "OPPORTUNISTIC" IS OFTEN USED as a blanket condemnation of a nonprofit organization. The implication is that the organization simply drifts from one field of activity to another, depending on the projects that happen to float into their field of vision. But the term disguises more than it reveals. Good nonprofits are adept at seizing unexpected opportunities, even those that might seem at first glance to be slightly askew from their core mission and agreed-upon strategy. If there is in fact a deep congruence between the new opportunity and the underlying objectives of the organization, the leaders need to educate people to the connection rather than assuming they understand. Clear, consistent communication is the best defense against the simplistic charge of "opportunism." [*Also see* "Donor-Driven."]

151

Other Peoples' Faiths, Learning from

 MAYBE YOU'VE DISCOVERED a philosophy, world view, or religion that works for you. Congratulations! Your opportunities to learn are just beginning. Be on the lookout for useful ideas, values, principles, and practices in philosophies, world views, and religions that you do *not* subscribe to. People who've never attended a Friends' service can find the Quaker practice of spiritual silence deeply enriching. Those of us (like me) who enjoy a glass of wine with dinner may find many of the teachings of Alcoholics Anonymous brilliant and worthy of study. Dedicated Creationists may find it profoundly moving to contemplate the scientific concept of the Big Bang.

The Outline of Your Speech Is Not Carved in Granite

 AN OUTLINE OF KEY IDEAS, facts, and stories is an essential tool for the speech maker. But it's a tool, not a straitjacket. Once you start speaking, vary from your outline based on how the audience is reacting. Linger on a point, take a tangent, or omit entire sections based on the needs of the moment as you see them from the stage. In other words, go in with a plan but be ready to modify it. (Notice that this is one advantage of speaking from an outline rather than a prepared text—it's easier to make changes on the fly.) The first time you improvise in this way, you may find it a bit intimidating. Don't worry—you'll get better at it, and more comfortable, with time and experience.

Overdress

IN RECENT YEARS, DRESS CODES in both work and social settings in the United States and many other countries have become more fluid and, in general, less formal. This can lead to some tricky decision-making for those who want to be viewed as leaders in their organizations. The best rule of thumb is to *slightly* overdress for every occasion. It's a way of subtly showing respect for your colleagues, friends, and others you may meet.

Overscheduling, Avoiding

 WHEN YOU'RE ON THE ROAD, it's tempting to allow yourself to be overscheduled in the name of "efficiency"—for example, by slotting in five or six donor or prospective donor meetings per day when visiting a city. Don't do it, and make sure your colleagues know you don't expect your days to be planned in this way. Better to focus on the most important meetings and leave some breathing room between appointments. This will give you and anyone traveling with you time to debrief and take notes in between meetings while the details are still fresh, and even start the follow-up process. This "down time" will also provide you with space for last-minute preparations for the meetings still to come and allow you to regroup mentally and emotionally.

Packing Tips for Business Travel

 WHEN PREPARING FOR A business trip, always pack one more set of underwear than you think you'll need. Also pack a bathing suit and exercise gear, even if you think you may not have the opportunity to use them—they take very little space and can provide you with some big benefits [*see* Exercise, Making Time to]. If you're going to check a bag while flying, also bring a Swiss Army knife—the multiple tools often come in handy when minor emergencies arise. Finally, consider packing any special seasonings or garnishes you like; having them on hand when you travel may perk up some bland airline or hotel meals.

Party, Throw a

 START A TRADITION OF THROWING a regular party— say, three times per year. It's a great opportunity to bring your growing network of friends, family, and colleagues together under your roof in a way that is enjoyable and deepens relationships. Make it fun, kid-friendly, and easy to prepare for and recover from. Have it catered, and don't promise more than you can fairly easily deliver. Schedule it when most people will find it convenient to come—Friday evening works well in many circles. And for best results, try to get some people dancing after dinner.

People—Three Kinds to Spend More Time With

 SPEND AS MUCH TIME AS possible around people who admire you, people you learn from, and people who make you laugh. When you must spend time with people at the other end of the spectrum—which we all must do occasionally—give yourself time to recover afterwards.

The Perfect Board, Don't Wait for

 AS A NONPROFIT LEADER, don't wait for your board of directors to "step up" as you hope they will before you invest a lot of time and energy in nurturing their commitment to your organization. That day will probably never come. Instead, start engaging with your board members *now* as if they *already* were the great board you hope they will become. Slowly but surely, they will respond to your support, encouragement, and guidance, in the process evolving into a team that is closer to your ideal board.

Perfectionism and Travel Planning

 WHEN PLANNING TIME AWAY from the office, you'll probably have dozens of details to organize. Don't stress yourself out by needing to get everything done perfectly before you depart. Good is usually good enough. Unnecessary perfectionism is likely to drive your friends, family, and colleagues crazy, undermining rather than enhancing your ability to perform at a high level during your trip.

Pessimists, Listen to the

A LEADER NEEDS TO BE realistically optimistic. But it's equally important to listen to the pessimists who work for and with you. Make a concerted, sustained effort to understand how your organization and its work are viewed by staff and board members who are worriers, alarmists, malcontents, or simply dissatisfied with the status quo. Recognize their concerns, acknowledge the germ of validity at the core of their complaints, and take appropriate actions to address them. Not only will this help you avoid excessive self-congratulation, it will ensure that you remain credible with the pessimists, retaining the support of people who might otherwise become serious thorns in your side or simply stop putting forth their best efforts.

"Please Clap!"

WHEN GIVING A SPEECH, don't be afraid to playfully ask the crowd to applaud when you've said something clever and noteworthy. This trick is especially effective if you use it after one person starts applauding and others do not immediately follow their lead. It will garner a chuckle as well as a round of applause. It will also help to relax you and the crowd while also giving you a moment to think about what you want to say next and how best to say it.

Post-Mortems—Why They're Essential

AFTER ANY MAJOR PROJECT or event is completed, you should schedule a post-mortem. Invite every member of your team who was involved (and perhaps others) to join an open, honest discussion about what went well, what didn't, and why, and the lessons for the future. It goes without saying that holding a post-mortem is equally important whether the project was a rousing success or a dismal failure. And as the leader, it's essential that you participate, and that you welcome divergent, unpopular, and "negative" views rather than driving them underground. This post-mortem discipline helps promote a true learning culture focused on continuous improvement.

Practice Cooking— Especially If You're "Too Busy" to Cook

 FOR MANY PROFESSIONALS with high-pressured jobs, cooking an evening or weekend meal can be something of a meditation, a way of shifting from the pressures of the work day to a more relaxing evening. If you're an inexperienced cook, keep it simple. Don't try to be a master chef. Instead, learn to prepare a few meals that are reasonably healthy and not too complex. Make big batches on the weekend that you can eat throughout the week. You'll find that each time you make a dish, the process of shopping for ingredients, doing the prep work, and the cooking itself become easier, especially as you discover patterns and short-cuts. Once you have four or five dishes that you know how to make easily and that you and the people you live with enjoy, you'll save money, be healthier, and celebrate a new skill.

Praise Your People Generously

 SOME LEADERS ARE SPARING with praise, fearing it may encourage people to become complacent. Most often, that philosophy is misguided. When your team members perform exceptionally well or succeed at tasks outside their comfort zone, don't hesitate to compliment them for it, using your best judgment as to whether to do it publicly or privately, orally or in writing. Accolades and recognition are also appropriate when people simply make a concerted effort or exceed modest expectations. In most cases, your praise will motivate people to do better, make them feel more secure with you, and enhance their sense of their own professionalism. It will also make them more receptive when you have to give them constructive criticism.

Preaching to the Choir—
Why It's Essential

 WHEN YOU HAVE HONED AN effective description of your organization's mission and its importance (as described in Messaging Change: The Four-Part System) don't fall into the trap of being reluctant to repeat this message to those who have heard it before—for example, your staff, your board of directors, and other key stakeholders. While the term "preaching to the choir" is popularly used to describe a communications effort that is unnecessary, there are actually very good reasons for doing it. Repeating your key message over and over, while varying the details and the illustrative examples, helps sustain and grow the commitment of your most devoted followers. Don't be afraid to do it.

Precedents, Setting

ONE BIG DIFFERENCE BETWEEN being the CEO and holding any other leadership role is that every decision you make as CEO has the potential to set a precedent for future decisions, purposefully or not. So be cautious about decisions you make, whether it involves the type and value of a gift you give a departing employee, the kind of equipment supplied to a staff member, or whether or not to give your team a week off with salary during the end-of-year holiday period. Once a precedent has been established, any future decision that deviates from it is apt to be viewed as unjust, regardless of your intentions.

Pre-Meeting Materials: Make Them Easy

 SENDING WELL-CHOSEN, RELEVANT reading materials in advance of a meeting can be very helpful in ensuring the participants are informed and prepared for the discussions. But keep the advance materials as clear and simple as possible. Try to deliver them at least seven days before the meeting (unless they are *very* short). Combine all the documents into a single email attachment rather than forcing people to download, open, print, and organize multiple documents. And arrange the materials in an order that matches the sequence of topics in the meeting agenda. All of these simple steps will help make it easy for people to participate in the meeting fully and enthusiastically.

Procrastination Pays . . . Sometimes

 IT'S GENERALLY A GOOD PRACTICE to respond quickly to people's calls, emails, and letters. It sends the messages that you are paying attention to people, that you care about them, and that you are decisive. *But* when a message touches on an issue that is complex, contentious, and emotion-laden—and especially when you find yourself reacting intensely to it—you should probably delay responding for a day or two. Use the extra time to seek advice and reconsider your immediate reaction. When applied to larger projects, this concept means that sometimes it is best to "muddle through" rather than make an impulsive decision or one that is simply not yet timely.

Profit Is Beautiful—Even for a Nonprofit

 WHEN LEADING A NONPROFIT organization, it pays to always be on the lookout for sources of *earned* revenue to supplement donations, government grants, or whatever other sources you most depend on (such as earnings on your endowment, if you are lucky enough to have one). This is especially important during times when you *don't need* the additional revenue—for example, when you are having success fundraising. That's when you have some discretionary resources to put into testing earned revenue ideas and investing in the infrastructure needed to turn them into reality. When the lean times return, you'll be glad you devoted time to building a profitable base to keep your organization afloat.

Proud of What You Want, Being

FOLLOW THIS THREE-STEP PROCESS in every area of your life: (1) Figure out what you want. (2) Become proud of wanting it. (3) Then work for it, which includes unapologetically asking for other people's help in getting it. Don't rush through the first step, and don't underestimate the importance of that second step. Being proud of what you want, especially if some people may see it as frivolous, indulgent, or just plain strange, can be difficult, but it's important. It is much easier to ask people for help if you are at peace with what you want. (Of course, if what you want is dangerous, unethical, or immoral, even if you can feel proud of it, you may want to rethink it.) My thanks to leadership expert Dave Ellis for first exposing me to this idea.

Public Speaking: The 10-Percent Rule

 WHEN GIVING A SPEECH, stay within the time limit you are given, plus or minus 10 percent. Thus, if you are allocated 10 minutes to speak, anything between nine and 11 minutes is all right. Notice that most speech makers don't follow this rule, which means that sticking to it will distinguish you as someone who is disciplined and respectful of your audience and those who invited you. This magnifies your influence. Until you are experienced enough at the podium to gauge the passage of time intuitively, use a stopwatch or clock to help you stick to this rule. Bonus tip: Avoid starting your speech by casually remarking, "I'll be brief." Generally, any remarks that last for more than three or four minutes are *not* considered brief, so if you say this and then speak longer, your audience is likely to feel that they've been misled.

Pull the Trigger Already

 IF YOU'RE LIKE THE VAST majority of managers, by the time you are seriously contemplating whether you need to fire someone, it is probably long past time for you to do so. The chances are high that the person on your radar screen has been quietly dragging the organization down for some time. Of course, you should listen to your legal or human resources team, who may counsel delay. But in many cases you will be well served by overruling their advice or at least moving faster than they would prefer. So get it over with. Your colleagues will likely appreciate your decisiveness, especially those who have been devoting their own time and energy to covering for the incompetence of their teammate. And then make sure you handle the dismissal in the most humane and professional way possible [*see* Kryptonite Against an "Unfair Dismissal" Lawsuit].

Question, Just Answer the

 ONE OF THE CHALLENGES OF leadership is balancing the need to appear strong and self-assured with the need to be open to challenges and criticism. Here's a subtle bit of communications strategy that has helped me. When someone asks a challenging question, especially if it implies criticism that you believe is unfair or uninformed, don't feel compelled to go beyond the specific question in your response. For example, suppose someone asks, "Did you run this report by so-and-so before you released it?" It's easy to assume that this question carries the implied demand, "If you didn't, why not?" But don't respond as if that additional question has been asked. Stick to the original question: "No, I didn't send it to them." Anticipating and responding to further questions—and perhaps the criticisms they imply—only makes you appear insecure and defensive.

Question, Repeat the

 DURING THE Q-AND-A SESSION following a speech, it's often useful to briefly summarize an audience member's question before answering it. This serves at least three purposes. (1) It ensures that everyone in the audience has heard the question. (2) It allows you to subtly frame or clarify the question to make it as relevant as possible to the mass of listeners. (3) It gives you an extra ten seconds or so to think about your answer before providing it.

Reaching Out to Others When Crisis Strikes

 Every organization experiences times of extreme stress. When this happens, some leaders tend to hunker down, turning inward and trying to struggle through the crisis on their own—a strategy that usually proves counterproductive. (Trust me—I took that path too many times early in my career.) Instead, when crisis strikes, renew your connections with others. Start by figuring out what you did to help cause the problem, and let people know that you recognize that you played a role. Then think about others who are impacted by the problem or may feel responsible for causing it, and say and do whatever you can to make them feel better. They will remember and appreciate the fact that you thought about them in that moment of darkness—and they will be more likely to provide their fullest support in helping to solve the problem.

Recognizing Donors, Flexibility in

 WHEN IT COMES TO PUBLIC recognition for their gifts, financial supporters of nonprofit organizations are all over the map. Some relish being praised in public; others prefer anonymity; still others are most comfortable with low-key or private recognition from someone they respect. The only rule is to not make any assumptions. Ask donors about their preferences, and don't take for granted that they will initially express those preferences with complete candor—for example, some people hunger for public acknowledgment but feel shy about asking for it. So you may need to ask multiple times, and try to create an atmosphere in which donors will feel comfortable about discussing how they really feel.

Recycle Your Best Messages

 MOST OF THE PRESENTATIONS, memos, reports, and speeches that you deliver as a leader will be routine events: They'll communicate your message about the mission of your organization with reasonable effectiveness, and your audience will come away having learned something useful. But once in a while, you'll hit a home run—and you'll know it by the smiles on people's faces, their rapt attention, and the compliments they offer you later. When this happens, look for opportunities to spread the message further. Integrate it into your basic stump speech. Then consider turning it into an op-ed column for your local newspaper, an opinion piece for an industry magazine, or a blog post for your organization's website. For most communicators, moments of triumph are rare—rather than waste them, milk them for all they are worth!

Renters and Owners: You Need Both

 IN A MISSION-DRIVEN ORGANIZATION, some employees are renters who intend to stay and contribute for a few years while they build their resumes, after which they'll move on. Others are owners—some call them "true believers"—who want to settle in for a long time, relating to the organization more or less as if *they'd* founded it. Strive to have at least one third of your middle and senior management be owners. Build on their deep commitment, and forgive their faults. Owners are highly valuable. But renters are important, too. Sometimes they can see the organization's flaws more clearly than owners. Renters may be more willing to talk about those organizational flaws openly, since they plan to leave some time anyway. So strive for a healthy mix of both renters and owners—your organizational culture will benefit from it.

Repair the World—At Least a Tiny Bit of It

 WHETHER YOU'RE ON THE JOB or just living your life, get into the habit of continually looking for ways to make your society a little better. If you see a need that you can help to address, push through the inertia and other barriers and get it done. Reinforce this frame of mind by doing little things to improve your community every day—even something as small as noticing a piece of trash on the sidewalk, picking it up, and putting it in the next garbage can you see. [*Also see* "Giving at the Office": Why It's Not Enough.]

Respond to Gifts Quickly

 THE SPEED WITH WHICH YOU respond to donations speaks volumes about your organization. One of the things that most screams "poorly run nonprofit" the loudest is failing to deposit a donor check within one to two business days of receiving it. Another is not sending a gift receipt for tax purposes within two to three business days. For a larger gift, you will also want to send a personalized thank-you note—but don't delay the gift receipt until you come up with the perfectly worded thank-you message. Send it out right away!

Reward Failure

 EVERY LEADER KNOWS YOU should reward success. But there are times when it is just as important, if not more important, to reward failure. When a team member shows that they have learned a profound lesson from a mistake or setback and have emerged a stronger professional as a result, give them *more* responsibility, not less. Doing so will demonstrate that you encourage risk-taking and that you recognize and honor growth. You'll also likely create a team member who is extra loyal and eager to prove that your faith in them is well placed.

Ritual, The Value of

 IF YOU LEAD A GROUP THAT will be meeting periodically, consider implementing a ritual that is distinctive to the group. You can suggest one or solicit ideas from other members. This can be a good way to build cohesion and shared purpose as well as to deepen relationships among members. Some possibilities include an opening prayer (perhaps drawn from a different faith tradition each time), a moment of silent reflection, a dramatic reading, a check-in moment for each member to describe something special they've done since the last meeting, or even singing a song together. Don't assume that your team members are "too sophisticated" for such rituals—most people enjoy them, especially after they've participated a few times and become accustomed to them.

Role Model, Learning from a

 WE ALL HAVE ROLE MODELS that we mostly respect from afar—directors of organizations to which we don't belong, spokespeople and leaders of causes adjacent to our own. Occasionally you may get the opportunity to directly observe them doing what they do best. When this happens, get every bit of value you can from it. "Put your big ears on," jot down notes about what you observe, and try to distill learnings from the experience. Later you may want to write about the experience—just for your own benefit, or for sharing with colleagues or an even broader audience if appropriate [*see* Big Ears—What They Are and How to Use Them]. The wisdom and examples of the best among us are precious resources not to be wasted.

Root Causes, Getting at

 ONE OF THE MOST COMMON leadership failings is misdiagnosing the cause of a problem by focusing on secondary issues rather than taking the time to dig down to root causes. For example, you may think you lack adequate staff due to the fact that your fundraising efforts for the year have fallen short, when in reality the core problem may be (for example) a failure to place the right people in the right roles or your use of outmoded technology. Never jump quickly to address a problem. Instead, pause to ask a series of *Why* questions that can help you get closer to the heart of the problem.

Rules for Board Members— How Strict Should You Be?

 ONE OF THE TRICKIEST CHALLENGES for the nonprofit leader is managing the (often sizeable) egos and expectations of board members. You'll want to establish some clear norms and expectations for board members (for example, regarding financial contributions and attendance at meetings), and your goal should be to apply them across the board. Once you start making exceptions, you can easily end up with a caste system, in which some board members play by one set of rules while others play by a different set— or by no rules at all. That's bad for team spirit and morale. However, as a practical matter, on rare occasions you may need to quietly bend a rule to accommodate a particular board member. If and when you do, you need to try to prevent this from becoming a troublesome precedent.

Sabbatical, The Benefits of a

 IF YOU'RE A LONG-TIME leader of an organization, the time may come when you realize you need a significant break—a sabbatical or long vacation. This kind of break can be very valuable for you as a professional. But it can also be beneficial for your organization. Stepping away from the reins of leadership and truly putting someone else in charge temporarily (rather than trying to retain control remotely) allows colleagues to step forward as leaders in new and exciting ways. As a result, everyone can grow, with long-term results that may be exhilarating and transformative for all.

Samaritan, Be a Traveling

TRAVEL CAN BE STRESSFUL, difficult, at sometimes even frightening. You may occasionally encounter a fellow traveler who is in trouble—someone who is lost and confused, who has been robbed, or is being bullied. When this happens, do what you can to help (without exposing yourself to needless danger, of course). You will feel good about yourself, and the travel gods will repay you many times over. And if you fail to act, you may be haunted by it for a long time.

Savoring Victories

 TAKE TIME TO SAVOR EVERY great moment in your life. It could be a public triumph, like receiving a prestigious award, or a significant internal achievement, such as upgrading your fundraising software or completing the annual audit (the kind of quiet victory that often goes overlooked in a nonprofit organization). In our ultra-busy lives, it's all too easy to rush past a notable success with a hasty, "Great!—Now back to work." You may even be afraid that enjoying an accomplishment too much will make you complacent or self-satisfied, dulling your drive to achieve more. In my experience, that doesn't happen. In fact, almost the opposite is true. Failing to savor great moments is almost as harmful as wallowing in despair when things are difficult. Over time, both of these dysfunctional responses reduce our ability to strive and grow.

Script, Tearing Up the

YOU MAY BE VERY CONTENTED with your career in the social or nonprofit sector. But it's a useful exercise to occasionally imagine tearing up the script and radically changing your career. Picture yourself moving out of your leadership role, out of the organization you lead, and even out of the social sector. Maybe you will conjure up a pathway that intrigues you, in which case you may want to take a few steps to investigate it. Perhaps this will lead to a wonderful new phase in your career. But most likely you will end up remaining where you are. If so, you may come to better appreciate how good you have it where you are, thereby sparing yourself some of the unhelpful self-pity that most leaders experience from time to time. In either case, your imaginary journey down a brand-new career path will have taught you something worthwhile.

Self-Affirmation

 MOST PEOPLE FEEL A LITTLE blue from time to time. For me, it tends to happen roughly once a week, and it may last for a couple of hours or even an entire day. A good antidote is to spend a few minutes immersing yourself in something that helps you recall what you are like when you are at your best. It could involve re-reading a letter or email from someone complimenting you, paging through something powerful or influential that you've written, talking to someone who admires you, watching a video of yourself performing well, or even just thinking about a time when you were productive, successful, and fulfilled. These kinds of self-affirmations provide a healthy reminder that your feeling of melancholy is temporary, and they may even lift you out of your temporary funk entirely.

Self-Pity, Avoiding

 MAKE A CONSCIOUS EFFORT to avoid the lazy trap of talking about the hardships you experience in your life and work. Cocktail-party or neighborhood-barbecue chatter about topics like long work hours, the tedium of conferences, or the inconveniences of frequent travel can easily degenerate into a self-pity session. Not only is this unattractive, but when self-pity is indulged by people who are objectively quite privileged (as most nonprofit leaders are), it can gradually blind us to the extent of that privilege, making us at least marginally less effective at advancing our missions. Instead, experiment with alternatives that guide the talk away from self-pity and in a more positive direction— for example, starting a conversation with the question, "What are you grateful for?"

Share Your Friends' Interests

 FRIENDSHIP IS A VALUABLE resource that busy professionals too often neglect. A great way to maintain and expand your rapport with friends is to actively participate in the things that interest them, something I first learned from my college pal Rohit Bakshi. For example, attend a meeting of a group they support; listen to a CD of their favorite band; visit a museum they love; or watch a movie they've recommended. Then let your friends know that you've followed up on an interest of theirs. They'll appreciate it, and your friendship will grow even deeper as a result.

Shoes, You'll Never Forget Your

 WHEN TRAVELING, IF YOU'RE nervous about the possibility of leaving something important at home or in your hotel room—your phone charger, your passport—eliminate this possibility the night before. Leave the essential item very close to or, better yet, inside something you absolutely cannot leave without—for example, your shoes.

Sleeplessness, Making the Best of

 TRAVEL HAS A WAY OF wreaking havoc on our sleep cycles. You've probably experienced arriving at your hotel room after a multi-hour flight to find yourself absolutely unable to get to sleep as the wee hours tick away. Don't just lie there, tossing and turning; the more you try to force yourself to sleep, the greater your anxiety will become. Instead, take advantage of your enforced wakefulness by catching up on work or reading a book. You'll be tired the next day, but you'll have gotten something productive done and will surely get a solid night's sleep after that.

Slow Down

 WHEN GIVING SPEECHES, most people talk too fast. Maybe the reason is nervousness, maybe it's the fact that the content of the speech is so familiar to them that they feel no need to linger on complicated concepts, subtle details, or essential points. Slow down. Give your audience an opportunity to absorb your message and to think about how it applies to them. And when you have something especially important to say, slow down even further for emphasis: a dramatic pause can be powerful. When you use this technique, try to look some members of the audience in the eye while you pause. If you have been roaming the stage, stay put for a moment. Let the anticipation build for what you will say when you resume.

Small Steps, The Power of

WHEN YOU ARE STUCK professionally, emotionally, or in a relationship, identify one or two easy, fun, and/or mind-expanding things that you can try to break out of the impasse, even in a small way. Then take those small steps. This can be a great way to restore your self-confidence and develop a bit of positive momentum you can build on.

Someone May Be Watching

ONE OF THE OLDEST self-administered tests for ethical behavior is still one of the most useful: Every time you are considering doing something wrong, even if it is relatively benign like telling a white lie, imagine that someone is putting you to a character test and observing closely what you choose to do. Not only is this a powerful way of drawing a clear line between right and wrong, it has the merit of being true: In this age of social media, it's entirely possible that someone may observe, judge, and spread stories about even your smallest actions. For the leader of a mission-driven organization, being mindful of this possibility and its potential impact on your reputation is particularly important.

Souvenir Shopping

 WHEN TRAVELING FOR WORK, don't feel obligated to buy gifts for your spouse or life partner unless there's some special reason to do so. Get home faster, rest more, and save your money instead. And if there are young children waiting for you at home, you'll find they're usually delighted to receive small, simple items you can easily pick up on your travels—hotel pens or stationery, airline tchatchkes, and the like.

Speak *Your* Truth

AND SPEAK IT BOLDLY. But don't confuse it with *the* truth.

Speaking Ill of the Departed

 DON'T GET INTO THE HABIT of verbally criticizing former colleagues who've left your organization, and don't allow those you work with to do it, either. It's bad form for several reasons: It suggests contempt for people who dare to leave "our team"; it risks poisoning relations with someone who may one day return to the fold or serve as a valuable external partner or ally; and, above all, it isn't fair, since they are not there to defend themselves. Of course, it's okay to discuss past projects and to mention factually what a former colleague may have done or failed to do in that connection. But avoid gratuitous recounting of former employees' mistakes. Otherwise you'll probably find yourself one day wondering how your old colleagues are now talking about *you*.

Speeches, High-Stakes and Low-Stakes

 OF COURSE, IT'S ALWAYS GOOD to prepare for any speaking opportunity. But calibrate your level of preparation and rehearsal with the magnitude of the opportunity for impact on your organization's goals and your personal profile. For a major speech, begin preparing a few weeks in advance if possible. Rehearse your speech in private, then revise your outline during the 24 hours before you go on stage. This allows you to catch and rework awkward or unclear formulations and to experiment with word choices that are clearer, more poignant, funnier, and flow better. For speaking opportunities where the stakes are not as high, a less-intense preparation process is appropriate. These are great opportunities to try out new stories, arguments, and techniques, and observe how people react.

Start with Your Conclusion

 IN MANY TYPES OF PUBLIC speaking, it works better to *start* with your conclusion (that is, your bottom-line message), rather than slowly building up to it over the course of your presentation. This strategy puts your audience at ease, since they know where you are going. Even those afflicted with short-attention-span syndrome—an ever-growing number these days—will be able to follow your speech, because the relevance and purpose of every anecdote and detail will have been made clear from the beginning.

Statistics + Stories = Persuasion

 WHEN SPEAKING OR WRITING about your organization, always try to interweave impressive statistics together with powerful, emotionally compelling stories. The statistics represent the hard data that demonstrate the value of your efforts; the stories bring to life the human dimensions of your work and tickle the imagination. Rather than relying on either statistics or stories alone, use both, and thereby touch both the heads and the hearts of your audience.

Stay Mad

MANY OF US IN THE NONPROFIT world got engaged with a particular problem because of an intense sense of outrage about it and a passion for fixing it. But when you work on a problem day in and day out, your outrage and your passion may begin to wane. When that happens, you have two options: You can find another line of work, or (much better) seek out and engage in activities that rekindle your sense of commitment. They might include mentoring others or being mentored, spending more time "in the field" (in other words, with those directly impacted by the problem you seek to address), or simply exposing yourself to the problem in new and different ways. Whatever you do, don't settle for merely going through the motions at work—mission-driven leadership is too important for that.

Stop Talking

 ONE OF THE HARDEST BUT most essential lessons for a new fundraiser to learn involves the power of silence. After you ask someone for money in a fundraising meeting, shut up. Just be quiet, and let them speak next. The resulting silence may feel awkward, but it's a pregnant pause during which a lot of thoughts and feelings are percolating. Let it happen. The conversation that follows will be important and, hopefully, fruitful and rewarding for everyone. It may not happen if you jump in too quickly.

Strike While the Fundraising Iron Is Hot

 FUNDRAISING STRATEGY requires thoughtful planning, especially when a big and potentially lucrative relationship is in the balance. But when combined with anxiety or self-doubt, the need for careful preparation can morph into an excuse for delay. Analysis paralysis and procrastination are marks of a mediocre, risk-averse, and unconfident fundraiser. Instead, strive to be action- and results-oriented. Move toward finalizing a donation before the lead gradually goes cold.

The Structure of Your Board—Why It's Overrated

 IN THE NONPROFIT WORLD, issues of board structure are often hotly debated. In particular, there are fierce arguments regarding the optimal number of members and the value of term limits. I think both issues are overrated. There are many small boards whose members wish they were larger, and many larger boards whose members wish they were smaller—without understanding that both sizes have their benefits and pitfalls. The same applies to boards with and without term limits (though I generally oppose term limits, despite the consensus among nonprofit experts that they are essential). Don't get bogged down in these issues. Instead, invest your energy in finding great board members and managing the group to elicit the greatest possible engagement and contribution from them.

Strut Their Stuff, Letting Board Members

IF YOU HAVE ONE OR A FEW board members who are particularly engaged in the organization—a member who may have helped to design, fund, and launch an effective program, for example, or one who has used their professional expertise to help educate and develop some of your staff members— try to create structured opportunities for them to show off their accomplishments to their peers. This can help spur friendly competition, increasing the board's overall level of involvement and the degree to which the members seek to contribute intellectually, not just financially.

Suck It Up and Show Up

 DON'T BE THE KIND OF leader who commits to meet with colleagues, give a presentation to an industry working group, or speak at a conference, and then shows up late or unprepared, or cancels altogether. Develop the discipline of showing up on time, doing your homework, and having something worthwhile to share. And don't call in sick just because you've changed your mind, found something better to do, or have a case of the sniffles. Suck it up and show up!

Text, Speak Without a

 WHEN GIVING A SPEECH, avoid using a prepared text. Those who read speeches from a text (unless they are *very* skilled at doing so) usually sound formal, boring, and disengaged. As a result, the audience often tunes out. Instead, create a one-page outline that simply lists the key ideas you want to convey, together with a few words to remind you of the favorite illustrative stories or examples you plan to use. You can jot notes in the margins of your outline if good ideas pop into your head, even just minutes before you begin speaking. The only exception to the no-text rule would be a quotation or some other material that must be stated with perfect accuracy.

"Thanks for That Lesson!"

 WHEN YOU LEARN SOMETHING from someone—even something little—let them know, and tell them that you appreciate it and, unless it is perfectly obvious, explain why. Don't assume that hearing such feedback won't matter to them. It probably will—and maybe much more than you think possible.

Three Phases of Board Membership

 MOST BOARD MEMBERS GO through three phases: (1) orientation, (2) high engagement and contribution, and (3) coasting. Your goals should be for them to get through orientation quickly—which will require effort on your part; to make the period of high engagement and contribution as long and productive as possible; and then to tactfully ease them off the board when they hit the coasting phase, while making some modest effort to keep them involved as board alumni.

Top Ten List, Your Personal

AS YOU GO THROUGH LIFE, keep a running mental list of the ten non-family members who have had the most positive influence on you. Make sure that, at least once each year, you connect with each of these people and remind them of how much they mean to you. Will they appreciate the message? Probably more than you can even imagine.

Transcendent Moments

MOST PEOPLE OCCASIONALLY experience transcendent moments—moments of unexpected, inexplicable, and intense joy, fulfillment, or satisfaction. This may happen in your professional life or in your personal life, and it may occur a few times or only once or twice. When it does, don't let it pass without notice. Take the time to reflect on it and to capture those reflections as best you can. Write a page or two describing what you experienced. You may even want to consider publishing your reflections for others to appreciate and learn from, because transcendent moments are an important aspect of the human condition that almost all people think about, care about, and long for.

Travel Cheap

 As a NONPROFIT LEADER, you should of course never claim travel or entertainment benefits beyond those permitted by your organizational policies. But go further by practicing habits that are significantly more frugal than policy requires—for example, by staying with friends instead of in a hotel, or by using frequent flyer miles rather than a paid airline ticket. Your grant dollars will stretch further. Better still, others in the organization will notice—and some will follow your example.

Tribe, Finding Your

PRACTICALLY EVERYONE HAS a tribe—a group of people with whom they feel deeply comfortable and that brings out the best in them. Your tribe may not include people who are in a position to support your work or advance your career—in fact, they may have nothing to do with either one. But being with them nourishes you emotionally, psychologically, and spiritually. Once you find your tribe, make it a priority to remain connected to them, even if it takes a lot of time, effort, or money. Your career will benefit, and your heart deserves it.

Trust, Earning

GAINING, GROWING, AND keeping someone's full trust—whether they are a member of your organizational team, an external colleague or partner, a professional acquaintance, or a personal friend—is a never-ending process, professionally or otherwise. The more you take the process for granted and neglect it, the more they are likely to withhold from you. The more you work on the process, the more they will reveal to you and be vulnerable around you.

Two Minutes to Touch Base

 WHEN RUNNING A MEETING that lasts more than a few hours, close it with a quick around-the-room reflection. (For multiday meetings, do this at the end of each afternoon.) Turn to the person at your left and invite them to spend one to two minutes commenting on the day, its highs and lows, its accomplishments and failures, and their own emotional state. Then proceed counter-clockwise, inviting everyone in the group to take a turn reflecting. You'll go last, both commenting about where you are personally and acknowledging and referencing some of the things you've heard. This is a great way to wrap up one day's work and set the tone for a productive start to the next time the group gathers together.

Unchain Your Colleagues from Their Screens

 IF YOU ARE IN THE HABIT of sending emails to your colleagues on weekends and holidays, make it clear to them whether you expect a response before the next working day. On rare occasions, a true emergency may demand an immediate answer. But in general, it's better to let people know that you *don't* expect a response on a weekend or holiday, though you'll willingly receive one. And be careful you don't (wittingly or unwittingly) reward people who quickly answer those emails that you send when suffering from insomnia at three a.m. on Saturday night—for example, by giving them extra praise or attention. Rewarding people who give up their personal lives is tantamount to punishing those who don't—which is a definite no-no.

Underpaid, Appreciate the

YOUR ORGANIZATION MAY BE lucky enough to have a few employees who have stayed loyal to you beyond what would be in the best interests of their careers—people who are working for you for less than they could command on the open market. Try to figure out who those people are. Get to know their motivations—what it is about your organization, your mission, their relationship to a mentor, or their unique personalities that makes them willing to give you service above and beyond the call of duty. And never take them for granted. Go out of your way to compliment, reassure, support, appreciate, and listen to them. Give them a raise or promotion when you can. If you do these things, they may continue to work for you and give you their best efforts for a long time to come.

The Underutilized Board

MOST NONPROFIT
ORGANIZATIONS have boards
that don't work very well
[*see* The Dysfunctional
Nonprofit Board]. One
version of this dysfunction is the
underutilized board, whose members are
generally supportive of the CEO but don't
add very much value to the organization.
The shortfall is likely to be most acute—
and to be noticed most quickly—in the area
of fundraising. However, the problem of the
underutilized board often goes unnoticed
until there is some crisis, when it may give
rise to finger-pointing, mutual
recrimination, and lasting distrust. Head
this off by engaging and energizing your
underutilized board before a crisis strikes.
Look for projects that specific board
members can tackle enthusiastically as a
way of bonding them more closely with
your organization [*see* Matching Projects to
People].

An Unfamiliar Setting, Making a Speech in

 WHEN MAKING A SPEECH in an environment that's new to you—an open-air stadium, a vast hall in which your face is being projected on a 30-foot screen, or before an audience made up mostly of billionaires—expect to feel uncomfortable and more nervous than usual. It can help to simplify your remarks in order to remain as focused as possible, much as a batter in baseball shortens his swing by choking up on the bat when the count runs to two strikes. Once you survive this unfamiliar context a single time, you will be more comfortable in such settings in the future.

Unlikely Attendee, Inviting the

WHEN YOU'RE PREPARING to celebrate a milestone event—a wedding, a major birthday or anniversary, a big achievement—there will be some people you'd love to have attend but whom you believe are unlikely to make it. Perhaps they live far away; perhaps they are very busy; perhaps age or infirmity makes travel difficult. Whatever the reason that might keep them away, go ahead and invite them anyway. At worst, they will be flattered. At best, they will surprise you by showing up, making your special day even more special.

Visible, Being

 YES, WE LIVE IN A WORLD where digital connections provide linkages among people no matter how many thousands of miles apart they may be. But being *visible* to your staff and your intended beneficiaries is still tremendously important. If you need to travel frequently, avoid working from home when you are not on the road, even if you really dislike commuting to your headquarters. Instead, spend as much time as possible in the office between trips. And when you are there, make an effort to be accessible: walk around, say hello to people, socialize with them during and after work, and eat lunch in the common area rather than at your desk. You'll be amazed as to how much more you will hear, see, learn, and understand simply as a result of being present in the flesh.

Wealth Secrets, Valuing and Keeping

 WHEN YOUR RELATIONSHIP with a key donor reaches a certain point, you may find that your benefactor starts revealing unexpected information about their wealth to you. This is a signal that they value their connection with you and that they trust your discretion implicitly. It may be appropriate to share some of this information with others in your organization in order to inform future fundraising efforts. But above all, never let it leak to any outside individual or organization, no matter how tempting the occasion.

When in Doubt, Ask for More

 FUNDRAISERS ARE MUCH MORE prone to ask for too little than for too much. This applies especially to inexperienced fundraisers, who often fall into the trap of caring more about making the donor feel comfortable than about advancing their organization's mission. The truth is that people are rarely offended by an overly aggressive ask, especially when it is made in the right spirit and doesn't appear manipulative or desperate. Most often, donors on the receiving end of funding requests beyond what they can do feel flattered and end up increasing the amount they had planned to give you. Bonus tip: If you find it intimidating to ask someone for, say, a million dollars—an amount larger than you yourself could probably ever afford—then ask your donor to "consider" donating that amount. For some people, including me,

that slight adjustment helps make the words come out more easily.

When Your Friend Becomes a Donor

 SOMETIMES A DONOR OR prospective donor to your nonprofit organization is a personal friend from before they popped up on your organization's radar screen. When this happens, it's often best to let someone else manage the donor relationship. At a minimum, get a trusted colleague with knowledge of good fundraising practices to advise you. Otherwise, you run the risk of letting a personal agenda influence your professional agenda, possibly damaging both your friendship and your organization's fundraising efforts in the process.

"Who Are You Today?"

OCCASIONALLY YOU MAY BE called upon to facilitate a meeting among people you don't know, or know only slightly. In other cases, you must lead a meeting involving people you know well but whom you may not have seen for a few days or longer. Either way, this lack of familiarity with the attendees and their current state of mind can make your job harder. Do whatever you can to minimize the problem. Something is better than nothing: A few words of conversation before the meeting starts is not as good as an hour-long discussion a week earlier, but it is something. If you'll be working with people who have a public profile, read some of their speeches or writings in advance. Even a few minutes devoted to an ice-breaking "Getting to know you" exercise can help you gauge the mood of the room and guide the discussion more intelligently.

Win-Win Game, Fundraising as a

DON'T THINK OF FUNDRAISING as taking something away from someone else. That's a disempowering mentality based on win-lose or zero-sum paradigms whose vision of the world is fundamentally inaccurate. Instead, think of fundraising as the art of brokering transactions where everyone gets something of value and comes out ahead.

Work/Life Balance

WORK/LIFE BALANCE IS an elusive, much-discussed goal for most professionals. Don't let anyone else dictate what work/life balance means for you. And don't fall into the trap of thinking it's a simple matter of hours in the day devoted to your job. Instead, it's a multi-factor equation that includes all the things that compete for your time, your energy, and your soul. Find a balance that works for you, even if it's very different from the way other people operate. Then continually reassess that balance, adjusting it as your needs, desires, goals, and energy levels change. And in your organization, create a flexible approach to work/life balance issues that recognizes how different each individual is.

Worries—Choosing Them Sensibly

EXPEND YOUR TIME, energy, and bandwidth worrying about things you can control: how you drive, the number of fundraising phone calls you'll make next week, or how you'll allocate next year's organizational budget. Don't waste those same resources worrying about things you can't control: the safety of your next airplane flight, the openness of your biggest donor to doubling next year's contribution, or how the stock market will perform.

You, It's Not About

WHEN SOMEONE TELLS YOU about a painful or traumatic situation they are going through, either professionally or personally, resist the temptation to share a similar story from your own life. You may think this would show empathy, but in reality it comes across as narcissistic and unhelpful. Instead, listen attentively, signal that you are comfortable with their emoting if they want to, and finally, simply ask, "Is there anything I can do to be helpful to you now?"

Zero-Sum Thinking, Why You Should Avoid

 As an organizational leader, you'll sometimes be confronted with a problem that seems to demand zero-sum thinking—a situation in which the gain to be enjoyed by one person or group seems inevitably counterbalanced by an equal loss suffered by someone else. You may find yourself thinking that your only option is to pick a winner and a loser—but before you do, pause and question your mental model of the situation. Sometimes, after thought and reflection, and with help from others' input, you may be able to transform the zero-sum dilemma into a win-win scenario. But don't use this as an excuse to prolong decision-making endlessly.

And One More Thing . . .

AS YOU GO THROUGH LIFE, making mistakes, discovering new truths, rediscovering old ones, and gradually uncovering what works for you and what doesn't, create your own list of lessons learned. Then pass it on . . . just as I've passed my list on to you.

Acknowledgements

THE CONTENT FOR THIS VOLUME was drafted during the process of writing *Changing the World Without Losing Your Mind*, during a period when I had a different vision for that book. I always knew that I wanted to publish this material in some form as a practical gift to future generations of changemakers, but was unsure how to do so until my publisher and editor Karl Weber proposed this project. I am grateful to him for all the big and little things he did to bring this book to market and make the process easy and enjoyable for me.

Jodi Waxenberg, the wife of my dear friend David "Waxy" Waxenberg, who departed this earth far too soon; Jony Melrod, someone I have known since my college days; and Brooke Raymond all worked untold hours editing this manuscript. These three friends believed in this book and put in a humbling amount of volunteer labor to bring it to fruition. Sam

Daley-Harris provided timely and helpful feedback on the introduction.

Rob Gailey's encouragement to complete this book was vitally important. Mona Bentz helped me better articulate how to describe what this was intended to be. Suzanne Orchard, the owner of Key West Island Books, helped convince me that there was a market for something like this, even in a tropical paradise where romance novels and mysteries are her stock in trade. My friends Joel and Donna Nelson were generous in letting me spend time with them in Key West in order to write, enjoy music, and let off steam—so much so that it often felt as if their home was my own.

The lessons contained in this book were influenced by hundreds of people. Those whose fingerprints are the most prominent are John Anderson, Ajay Banga, Tim Carter, Sam Daley-Harris, Susan Davis, Chris Dunford, Bob Eichfeld, Dave Ellis, Howie Erichson, Paul Maritz, Jennifer Meehan, Emalyn Mercer, Karen O'Malley, Michael and Chris Pascucci, Cedric Richner, Joan Robbins, Julian Schroeder, Muhammad Yunus, and my parents and step-parents.

My wife, Emily, has been both loving and supportive as I have shifted my focus in recent years to teaching, writing, and consulting. She never balked at the lifestyle changes that were required during this or any phase of my career. She remains my best supporter, advocate, advisor, and friend.

About the Author

ALEX COUNTS FOUNDED Grameen Foundation and became its president and CEO in 1997. A Cornell University graduate, Counts's commitment to poverty eradication deepened as a Fulbright scholar in Bangladesh, where he trained under Professor Muhammad Yunus, the founder and managing director of Grameen Bank, and corecipient of the 2006 Nobel Peace Prize. Since its modest beginnings, Grameen Foundation grew to become a leading international humanitarian organization.

Counts is the author of several books, including *Small Loans, Big Dreams: How Nobel Prize Winner Muhammad Yunus and Microfinance Are Changing the World,* and *Changing the World Without Losing Your Mind: Leadership Lessons from Three Decades of Social Entrepreneurship.* He has also written numerous articles in the *Stanford Social Innovation Review,* the *Washington*

Post, the *Chronicle of Philanthropy*, and other publications.

Today Counts is an independent consultant to nonprofit organizations, a professor at the School of Public Policy at the University of Maryland College Park, and an affiliated faculty of its Do Good Institute. He also serves as a member of the Advisory Council of the Center for Financial Inclusion and is an active Court Appointed Special Advocate (CASA) volunteer in Prince George's County, Maryland.

Also by Alex Counts

This down-to-earth guide to mission-driven leadership is based on Alex Counts's decades of experience as an acclaimed nonprofit leader. Counts offers practical advice on such vital activities as fundraising, team-building, communications, and management. He shows you how to run an organization—and your own life—both effectively and sustainably, giving joyfully to those around you while also caring generously for yourself.

Candid, funny, insightful, and wise, *Changing the World Without Losing Your Mind* is a book you'll refer to throughout your career . . . no matter where your mission may lead you.

One of *Forbes*'s 12 Must-Read Books for Nonprofit Employees • *Chronicle of Philanthropy*'s Editor's Pick among nonprofit books of 2019

AVAILABLE ON AMAZON, ON B&N.COM, AND AT BOOKSELLERS EVERYWHERE